VILLAGE
BUILDINGS
of BRITAIN

Matthew Rice

VILLAGE
BUILDINGS
of BRITAIN

FOREWORD BY
HRH The Prince of Wales

FOR EMMA BRIDGEWATER

First published in Great Britain in 1991 by
Little, Brown & Company, (UK)
Brettenham House, Lancaster Place
London WC2E 7EN

First paperback edition published in 1992
Reprinted 2001

Designed by Andrew Barron and Collis Clements Associates

ISBN 0-316-85688-6

A CIP catalogue record for this book
is available from the British Library

Printed in China by Imago

ACKNOWLEDGEMENTS

The author would like to thank the following
people for their invaluable help in the preparation of this book:

Andrew Cox
Jane Heyes
Alastair Langlands
David Linley
Mary McCarthy
Peter Rice
Emma Todd

and most especially
Edward Impey

CONTENTS

As Matthew Rice writes in his splendid introduction to this book, it is the responsibility of us all to ensure that vernacular traditions of building continue to nourish us in our treatment of old buildings, and our designs for new ones. These vernacular habits were far from naive, and were able to accommodate all sorts of pressures and changes within an approach to building which almost invariably produced something that felt "right".

The trouble nowadays is that so often any attempt at retaining a vernacular tradition is mercilessly denigrated as being "Disneyland". All I can say is that we must not allow ourselves to be put off by such derogatory comments, . . . As Matthew Rice says in his introduction, why on earth should "detailed designs of new façades *not* be copies of past styles?"

We can not be reminded enough of the profound "rightness" of the village buildings of Britain; perhaps in time we will learn to equal them. And it is with this in mind that I welcome a lovingly illustrated book of this kind. Would that Matthew Rice were able to produce pattern books of this kind for every town and city in Britain—it would give us all a standard to live up to in what we build in the future.

HRH THE PRINCE OF WALES

INTRODUCTION

N O ARCHITECT designed the variegated rows of cottages that characterize the villages of Britain. They are the work of generations of local builders working with materials and in styles with which they have been familiar since childhood.

These styles developed as one building imitated its predecessor, making use of the most readily available materials; stone, brick or wood, and using them in a fashion unique to that place. Every area of Britain, every county, almost every village, has its own idiosyncracies that root the houses firmly in their immediate environment. This is vernacular architecture.

For such a small country, Britain is remarkable in the variation of its building types. A major reason for this is the diversity of its geological formations. As the underlying rock changes from limestone to flint or from granite to sand, so the buildings change in appearance. Around the north coast of Norfolk houses are constructed of round grey pebbles, while the Cotswolds are endowed with buildings made of the wonderful honey-coloured limestone found locally. The presence of timber adds another dimension, although it rarely has the durability of stone or brick. Fine examples of half-timbered buildings survive, constructed with the traditional methods that endured right up until the eighteenth century. Weather too determines much about the style of buildings. In order to stand up to the westerly gales of the Hebrides the crofters' cottages are built of heavy granite and hug the ground, their turf roofs secured with hair-nets of rope.

The preservation of large country houses and their parks is a job undertaken by the National Trust and other bodies. However there is no co-ordinated effort to maintain our vernacular housing stock. This deficiency reflects the lack of importance attached to the vital business of conserving this part of Britain's inheritance. When designing modern housing, architects too need to have a clear understanding of this key part of our remarkable architectural heritage if regional identities are to be retained.

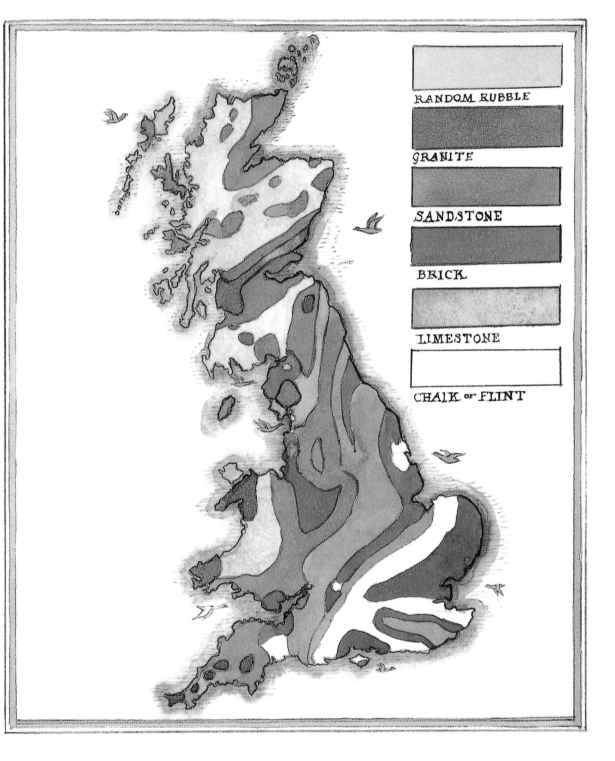

RANDOM RUBBLE

GRANITE

SANDSTONE

BRICK

LIMESTONE

CHALK or FLINT

A.

B.

C.

D.

Here is a house in four stages of restoration. At each stage another vital part of the character of the building is lost in the interests of 'improvement'. Worse still, the owner is under the illusion that he has been responsible for a sympathetic conversion.

Until the late eighteenth century the village was an agriculturally based, self-contained community. As well as farm workers, it included a number of craftsmen such as blacksmiths, cartwrights, coopers, basket and hurdle makers. Industry, such as it was before the Industrial Revolution, was also based in the country. Charcoal burners, potters, brewers and miners all had homes in the village, living and working with the farming community. Potters in the six small villages now known collectively as Stoke-on-Trent would work in the fields during the summer months and then return to their wheels and kilns for the rest of the year.

As well as labourers' cottages, larger farmhouses, workshops and a forge, a church, vicarage and perhaps a manor house, the village would include shops; a general store, a butcher and a bakery in which the whole village's baking would have been done. There would probably also be one or more pubs and maybe a windmill or watermill.

Dramatic social and economic changes during the last one hundred years have entirely altered the face of the British village. Agriculture has become mechanized and requires far fewer workers. A farm worked by twenty people at the turn of the century now only requires two or three men. Families have shrunk too and the number of dependants on an average farm is down from well over one hundred to about ten. The small industries have long gone and so too have most of the ancillary ones. The local school will probably have closed, the post office may be under threat, and the vicar, once at the very heart of the community, may now be spreading himself thinly between a number of different villages.

Vacant houses are bought by retired people, often from outside the area and by white-collar workers, many of them commuting to the cities for work or using the village as a weekend retreat. The demand for rural housing has pushed up the prices of property that was once almost worthless, forcing those agricultural workers who remain to move to council houses on the edge of the village. In this way the social infrastructure of the community is being destroyed.

Near large cities, the pressures to convert rural villages into suburbia have created an unprecedented threat to our vernacular housing stock. Many village buildings have been converted from their original working purpose to suit the

needs of the people moving in from the towns and cities. Vernacular architecture is now in the hands of those who do not understand it and unwittingly they may do great damage. They do not want a pigsty, vegetable garden, chicken run or stable. It is common for the small improvements and extensions made over several hundred years, the controlled disorder that marks the true vernacular building, to be demolished in two or three months and one person's view of a perfect country cottage imposed upon the long-suffering building. Not only are farmhouses and cottages at risk, there is hardly a shed, byre, barn or any other farm building which is not under threat of conversion. So often 'improvements' involve demolishing outbuildings, inserting inappropriate doors and windows and employing unsuitable modern materials, to say nothing of surrounding the building with neatly clipped lawns, kidney-shaped swimming pools and asphalt parking lots.

The problem is well illustrated in Otmoor near Oxford where two cottages face one another across a lane. One is a stone cottage nearly hidden behind apple and plum trees. Built from the local limestone, the house has windows that, although randomly placed, retain a sense of order and proportion. Geraniums fill the wooden casements on the ground floor windows and a large sash in the upper storey reveals a view through another window in what must be a wonderful sunny bedroom. The stone roof is sound although the ridge sags a little in the middle. It is a small house that has grown according to need; at various stages over the last hundred years lean-tos and a kitchen have been added, the fence repaired, the gate replaced and the trees pruned from time to time. It has developed the kind of patina that is so admired in antique furniture.

On the opposite side of the lane over a closely shaved hedge of cypress, (a tree better suited to Tuscany than Oxfordshire), stands its erstwhile twin, smarting under a coat of shining white paint. The windows have been taken out and replaced with double-glazed units that are stained a rich, treacly russet; not a treatment of wood traditionally used in the village, or indeed, anywhere else in Britain. It has been re-roofed in reconstituted stone, every line mathematically straight. The rambling garden has been ripped out and replaced by a neat lawn uncluttered by sheds or chicken coops. At the far end of the plot is a new garage

built of the same harsh, stained wood. The owners moved here from London because they yearned for the countryside and the charms of a village, but through well-meant but ill-advised improvements, no doubt considered as restoration, they have turned their part of it into the suburbia they left behind.

Development in Britain is controlled by the planning departments of the local councils which stipulate what can and cannot be done. In most areas councils now stress the importance of using local materials and following regional building techniques but these regulations are enfeebled because their remit does not extend to alterations to old buildings unless listed. These can be refaced, have their windows replaced and new porches added without planning permission. Councils also stipulate many very destructive conditions. For example insistence on the provision of off-street parking which often involves setting a house back from the road, a significant departure from traditional village planning. One council's leaflet offering advice on the design of new façades states that while they should reflect the prevailing proportions of surrounding buildings, they 'should not be copies of past styles'. Why on earth not? The whole question of local planning controls over village architecture needs reviewing. In the meantime home owners have tremendous power which could be used to good effect.

Traditionally, village houses line the street each house relating to, and frequently overlooking, another. Since the Second World War, however, there has been a move towards constructing groups of detached houses and the indiscriminate scattering of the bungalow, a building with roots not in the English countryside but in the tea plantations of Asia. Property developers have been allowed to build irresponsibly. Rather than integrating new housing piecemeal, they have favoured forming independent 'estates'. The superficial stylistic devices in these buildings appease conservationists in the planning department and the parish council, but 'Glebe Place' and 'Willow Way' (it might as well be 'Hazelnut Cluster'), are settlements which, like their banal names, have no roots in their community and are all too often simply cynical business ventures designed to capitalize on the city dweller's yearning for the countryside. Their isolation both from the rest of the village and from one another is socially divisive.

It is very important that the owners of village buildings genuinely understand local styles and use this knowledge when planning changes to their houses. Although books can lay down guidelines for conversion and renovation, choice of detail and material is best made by studying the windows, door mouldings and stonework of unmodernized houses nearby and preserving or imitating those styles and the materials as closely as possible. Wherever possible, windows, porches and doors should be custom made and not selected from the limited choice in a commercial catalogue. Perhaps most importantly owners should resist the temptation to do unnecessary work, to paint a house that has previously been left unpainted, to replace windows that could be mended or to fix double glazing to the outside rather than the inside of a window. Although often overlooked, the edges and environs of a cottage are as important as the building itself; the outbuildings and garden should be considered integral parts of the property and treated with a similar degree of respect.

Half a century ago it would have been hard to find a rural village in Britain that had been spoilt. Twenty-five years ago the countryside still looked very much the same as it had at the turn of the century. Now it is almost impossible to find a village which is not partially damaged by insensitive development and over-zealous restoration. Over the last decade there has been much discussion in the press about the concept of stewardship and of our responsibilities to preserve country houses, farms, woodland and hedgerows for future generations. This stewardship applies equally to the smallest cottage. We should think of ownership more as a tenancy than an absolute freehold. Positive steps must be taken to stem the damage our vernacular building is sustaining. Retaining a dozen 'museum' villages is not enough.

In an enlightened age, a constructive attitude to the conservation of villages should encompass responsible expansion with harmonious new building and a sensitive and well-informed approach to restoration. Happily this is a responsibility that falls on the individual householder or developer and not on government or local authority bodies. In this lies the greatest hope for Britain's vernacular architecture.

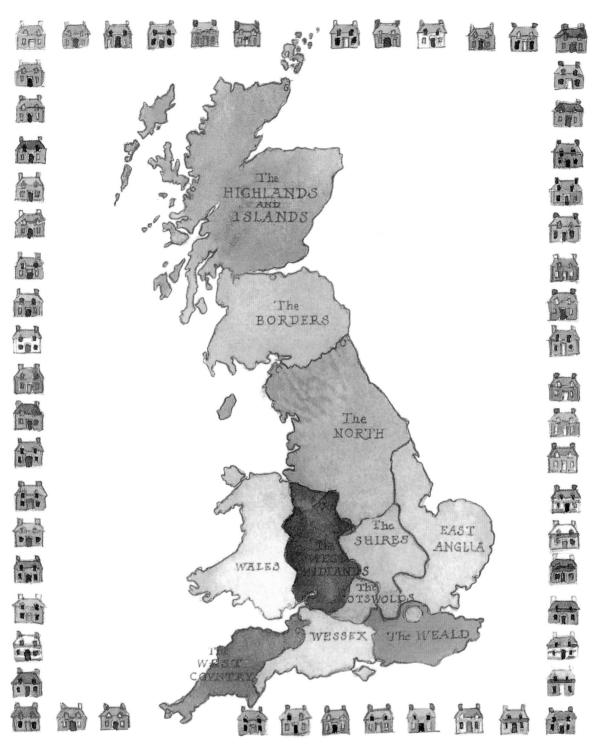

The
HIGHLANDS
AND
ISLANDS

The
BORDERS

The
NORTH

WALES

The
WEST
MIDLANDS

The
SHIRES

EAST
ANGLIA

The
COTSWOLDS

WESSEX

The WEALD

THE
WEST
COUNTRY

The WEST COUNTRY

SALTRAM · Devon

ILFRACOM

BUDE

CORNWALL.

PADSTOW

LAUNCESTO

CAMELFORD

Bodmin
Moor

R. Tam

BODMIN

NEWQUAY

ST AUSTEL

PLYMOUTH

ST IVES

R. Fal

PENZANCE

LANDS END

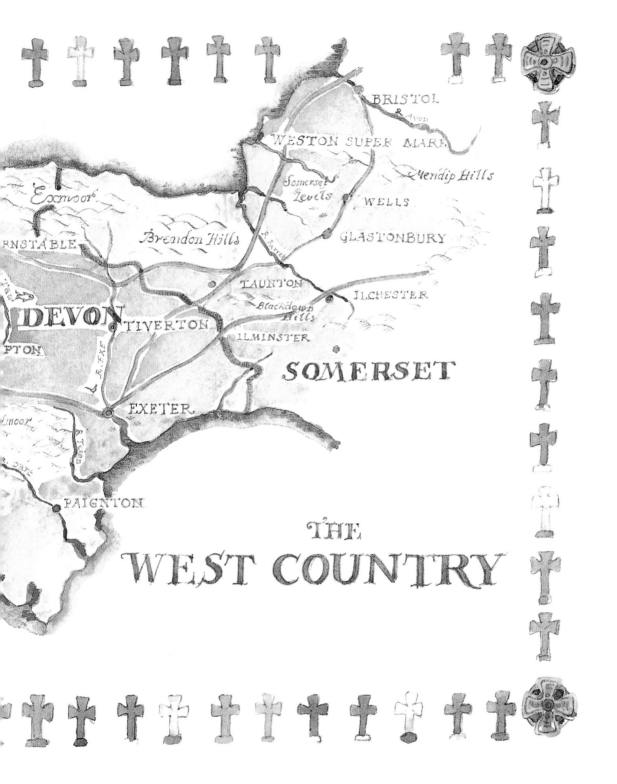

The WEST COUNTRY

DEVON AND Cornwall are now reasonably accessible from London and the rest of England as motorways grind across the country yet, in the south west, where almost no-one in the region lives more than twenty five miles from the sea, the powerful sea-faring tradition has shaped a distinctive and self-contained area. Sustained by the trade which its numerous ports attracted, by rich farmland and plentiful natural resources—tin and copper as well as granite in Devon and Cornwall and iron and lead in Somerset—the region has always been prosperous and independent.

The belt of oolitic limestone that runs from Yorkshire through the countries of Leicestershire, Northamptonshire, Oxfordshire and Gloucestershire continues southwards to the coast. Although the stone buildings of Somerset are less ostentatious in their decorations than those of the Cotswolds, the warm gold colour remains changing to a richer brown in the south of the county. One of the most impressive outcrops of limestone in Britain is at the Cheddar gorge in Somerset. This dramatic escarpment marks the edge of the limestone belt and is the easterly boundary of the Somerset levels. This low-lying, flat and often waterlogged part of the country stretches from Avonmouth to Devon.

In terms of building materials Devon is by far the most diverse of the western counties. Chalk and flint are abundant in the southern half, bricks are used in the north. There are pebble houses around the coastal areas and ample supplies of limestone, sandstone and granite are all present. More peculiarly this is the most concentrated area of cob building in Britain. Cob is a mixture of dung, mud and straw from which walls are made. Construction is a long process as each course has to dry out before another is added and a two-storey cottage may take up to two years to complete. Thus it is not surprising that this building method has died out to be replaced by rendered brick and breeze block. The houses are set on stone plinths to keep out the rats and the damp and are generally roofed with wheat or reed thatch. The completed buildings are then whitewashed and the windows and door frames frequently painted black.

In Cornwall many of the houses, which are generally made of stone, are similarly covered with layers of white or pale-coloured lime plaster rendering. Slate and granite are the main building stones, and buildings are usually capped with thatch or slate. A peculiarity of parts of Cornwall is the use of hung slate as a walling material, which makes a feature of the varying greens and greys of this stone. There is a clear unity about Cornwall but too much recent building has been harsh and ugly with no reference whatsoever to local traditions. The architectural legacy of the farmer who has replaced his flock of sheep with a gaggle of holiday chalets will be of debatable value to future generations.

NR TREGONY
CORNWALL

CREDITON
DEVON

NR WADEBRIDGE
CORNWALL

BICKENHALL
SOMERSET

CULLOMPTON DEVON

Nᵣ TAUNTON · SOMERSET

Nᴿ CARDINHAM CORNWALL

THE three counties which make up the West Country, Somerset, Devon and Cornwall, have a varied and idiosyncratic vernacular architecture. Like the long houses of Wales, many of the houses have chimneys at the front, as in the terrace at Cullompton, but they are narrower and more elegant than their Welsh counterparts and, although made of brick, they are plastered to match the walls. The combination of thatch and whitewashed or pale-coloured rendering used in this terrace and in the cottage at Tregony is a particularly pleasing one which characterizes many Devonian and Cornish villages.

The colour gradations of the granite of Devon and Cornwall make it visually more rewarding than the dark varieties found in Wales and prevent it from looking oppressive when used in large quantities as in the window at Tregony in Cornwall shown on the next page.

Slate is so widely available a building material that it is even used to create the retaining walls of the many banks that mark the boundaries, some of them neolithic in origin, of Cornish fields. It is used in a herringbone pattern to give extra strength, as in the example shown overleaf at Treyarnon. Slate can also be used in a much more precise architectural way as in the porch at Charlestown.

PADSTOW · CORNWALL

Nr ILMINSTER · SOMERSET

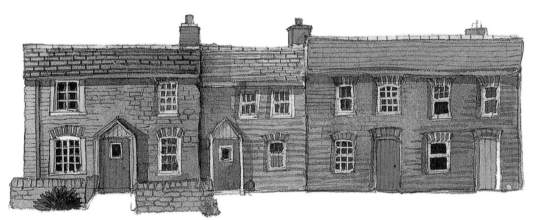

WADEBRIDGE · CORNWALL

TREGONY · CORNWALL

NETHER STOWEY · SOMERSET

TREYARNON · CORNWALL

PADSTOW · CORNWALL

CHEDDAR · SOMERSET

Nr ILMINSTER.
SOMERSET

TREGONY · CORNWALL

PADSTOW
CORNWALL

NORTH TAWTON
DEVON

St KEW 2½ HIGHWAY · LONGSTONE BODMIN 5 MILES

CHARLESTOWN

PORLOCK
SOMERSET

Nr CHEDDAR
SOMERSET

CULLOMPTON
DEVON

St AUSTELL
TO GRAMPOUND AND TRURO

A MERCHANT'S HOUSE in TIVERTON

An area of fertile and productive farmland, Devon has many beautiful market towns. This eighteenth-century house is a fine example of a wealthy merchant's attempt to aggrandise himself with architectural pretensions. It is possible that an architect was employed but more likely it was the work of the local builder whose knowledge of current architectural practice has taken it beyond the true vernacular. A sturdy five bay, two-storey pedimented building with an elevated cellar, it is built of red brick with rubbed brick lintels and has quoining and string courses of Portland stone. The most elaborate carving is centred around the doorway, which, topped with an elegant fanlight, is surrounded by a fine wooden porch with a curved broken pediment. This use of decoration is typical of the eighteenth century when even a relatively untutored builder would have had a strong grasp of the grammar of classical architecture.

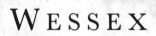

WESSEX

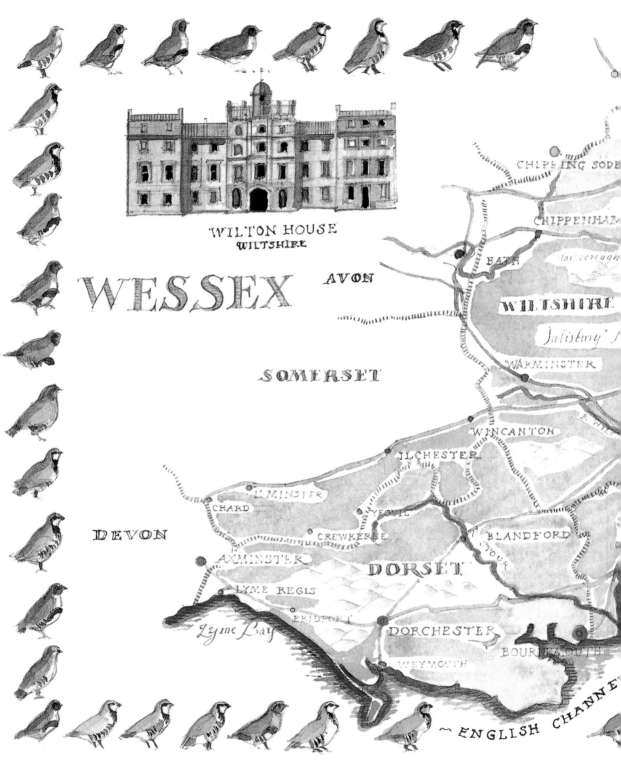

WILTON HOUSE
WILTSHIRE

WESSEX

AVON

SOMERSET

DEVON

CHIPPING SODB

CHIPPENHAM

BATH   Marlborough

WILTSHIRE

Salisbury

WARMINSTER

WINCANTON

ILCHESTER

ILMINSTER

CHARD   YEOVIL

CREWKERNE   BLANDFORD

AXMINSTER   STOUR

DORSET

LYME REGIS

BRIDPORT

Lyme Bay   DORCHESTER

BOURNEMOUTH

WEYMOUTH

~ ENGLISH CHANNEL

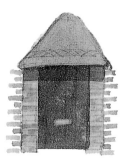

WESSEX

EFORE BRITAIN was a unified country, Wessex was its most powerful kingdom. Harold, who fell at the Battle of Hastings, was descended from the kings of Wessex, and Winchester and Salisbury boast two of the finest cathedrals in Britain.

Despite its proximity to London it remains an area of great beauty, but few parts of it are truly unspoilt and one is never far from a road. It suffers from its prosperity and there is hardly a cottage that remains unimproved, everywhere windows have been replaced and gardens suburbanized.

Most remote and probably best preserved is Dorset, a county of small market towns and villages. This is the setting for the novels of Thomas Hardy and its landscape would be familiar to him today.

From the fossil-infested cliffs of the Dorset coast, the belt of limestone that stretches to Yorkshire begins. Here the warm golden rock produces an easily workable building stone that reacts most satisfactorily to the changes in light.

Wessex is well wooded, particularly in the New Forest, and although timber-framed buildings are common they are not as dominant as in the neighbouring Weald. Brick, and an imitation of it known as mathematical tiles (see glossary), are more common.

Marlborough is typical of the towns of southern England. A broad main street that once housed the market is now lined with cars but on either side stand variegated rows of fine shops and merchants' houses made of brick, brick and flint, chalk and hung-tiles. With a large church at one end and the town hall at the other, the size of this elongated square is evidence of the agricultural wealth of the area.

This part of Wiltshire has been continuously inhabited since Neolithic times and evidence of this can be found along the ancient Ridgeway, most spectacularly at Stonehenge, whose massive megaliths are dwarfed by the juggernauts that plough by on the A303.

The current obsession with leisure is leading to increased conflict as more and more golf courses, theme parks, caravan sites and water parks threaten to spread across the countryside. While it is essential to provide access for an urban population, the developers urge to sanitize and package our rural heritage trivializes its traditions.

Further east and north the brick and flint villages between Reading and Oxford often seem surprisingly remote and some of the most beautiful brick building in Britain can be found in West Wycombe and Henley, Watlington and Nettlebed in the Thames Valley.

Further south, between Alton and Petersfield, lies an area of wooded hangers and hidden valleys traversed by single-track lanes so steep that they are frequently blocked in winter. The most beautiful of its villages is Selborne, home of the eighteenth-century naturalist Gilbert White, whose vivid diaries and correspondence describe an almost unchanged environment.

Nr PEWSEY WILTSHIRE

Nr PETERSFIELD·HAMPSHIRE

MARLBOROUGH·WILTSHIRE

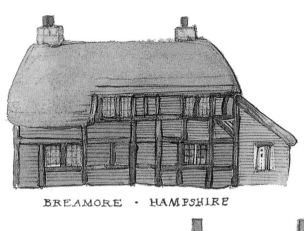

BREAMORE · HAMPSHIRE

MARLBOROUGH
WILTSHIRE

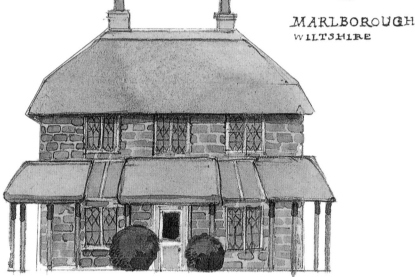

WINTERBOURNE CARNE
DORSET

Among the diversity of architectural styles and building materials seen in southern England, the chalk and the flint houses are the most characteristic. They often use brick for strength, for example in the chalk cottage near Pewsey where they are used around the door and window, while unusually the roof is made of slate. Brick and flint are combined in the Marlborough and Cherhill cottages.

Although there is not as much half timbering here in southern England as in the south-eastern counties, many examples, such as the seventeenth-century thatched house at Breamore in Hampshire, survive. The heavy stone roofs on the limestone outbuildings at Corfe Castle in Dorset cast exaggerated shadows and must really test the strength of the roof timbers. In contrast, the thatched verandahed house at Winterbourne Carne in Dorset exhibits a fine approach to local materials and forms, producing a pleasing combination of Regency and vernacular.

PETERSFIELD
HAMPSHIRE

Nʳ PEWSEY
WILTSHIRE

Nʳ PEWSEY
WILTSHIRE

CHERHILL
WILTSHIRE

CORFE CASTLE
DORSET

PETERSFIELD
HAMPSHIRE

MARLBOROUGH
WILTSHIRE

Windows, the eyes of a building, are of crucial importance. However fine the other elements and details of a facade may be, insensitive, unsuitably-designed replacement windows will mar the entire appearance.

Five examples are shown here. The fine eighteenth-century sash windows at Marlborough are elegant without being urban and ideally suit their position in a grand market town. They are set off well by the contrasting blue and red bricks of their surrounds. A simple and solid casement sits beneath the heavy roof slabs in the Corfe Castle dormer window while a sliding sash is a less common variation used beneath the thatched shelter of the old shop in Hambledon. A much simpler window with a plain curved brick lintel suits the small Petersfield house, and the leaded casements in the Marlborough gable are of the same size as the hung tiles that surround them.

The columned porch and door-case at Faringdon is an elaborate and impressive carved wooden entrance to a pub.

There is a very fine dividing line between negligence and the over restoration of a wall. The homogeneous combination of materials in Pewsey, Cerne Abbas and Okeford Fitzpaine (shown below) could so easily be ruined by inappropriate pointing or, worse, by painting. The colours of the flint, chalk, limestone and brick have aged together to produce an overall patina which must be preserved if the building is to retain its authentic character.

Nr PEWSEY
WILTSHIRE

CERNE ABBAS
DORSET

OKEFORD FITZPAINE
DORSET

CORFE CASTLE
DORSET

W·H·LANGTRY

HAMBLEDON　　HAMPSHIRE

Anno Dom 1632 October XI
William Wood

FARINGDON
OXFORDSHIRE

MARLBOROUGH
WILTSHIRE

The
ARTS and CRAFTS
MOVEMENT

Interest in the vernacular is not a new phenomenon; the mid-nineteenth century also saw a revival in traditional building crafts and techniques. Outraged by the shoddy quality of mass-produced goods spawned by the Industrial Revolution, the designer and philosopher William Morris aimed to return to the qualities and standards of pre-industrial England. The school of craftsmen and designers that gathered about him became known as The Arts and Crafts Movement.

continued overleaf

BUDLEIGH SALTERTON
DEVON
ERNEST GIMSON 1913

STEEP
HAMPSHIRE

ALFRED POWELL

STEEP
H. GIMSON

STEEP
UNSWORTH 1910

MARKFIELD
E. GIMSON · 1897

39

Morris was not an architect, but he did commission Philip Webb to design a house for him in the vernacular style. It was at the turn of the century that a second wave of his followers became much more involved in buildings. Ernest Gimson designed the cottages in Markfield and Budleigh Salterton, both almost academic essays in their respective local vernaculars, while his highly self-conscious re-working of traditional timber construction can be seen opposite in the covered way at Bedales. In the house at Froxfield, his follower Lupton was developing an idiosyncratic 'rural' style, a fusion of his own ideas with various vernacular traditions, an approach continued by Gimson's nephew Humphrey, in his design for the house at Steep. Alfred Powell's house at Steep, with its roofs sweeping almost to the ground, is also characteristic in its exaggeration of a traditional style.

In these buildings the architects prepared a total design not only for the elevations, walls, roof and chimneys, but for every catch, bolt and window and even the furniture inside. This amazingly thorough and high principled attitude is now sadly rare, however elements of it could so easily be revived today. Commissioning a local joiner to make a window frame or a mason to carve a finial can make a house remarkable and every time you reject the builders catalogue you are fighting the destruction of vernacular architecture.

FROXFIELD
HAMPSHIRE

BUDLEIGH SALTERTON
DEVON

BEDALES
HAMPSHIRE

KELMSCOTT OXFORDSHIRE

FROXFIELD HAMPSHIRE

PRIORS DEAN · HAMPSHIRE

The WEALD

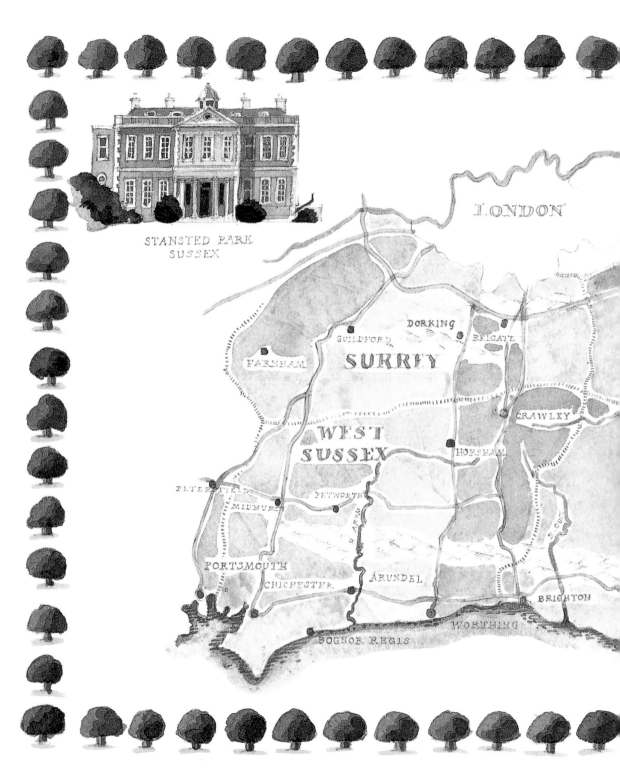

STANSTED PARK
SUSSEX

LONDON

SURREY

FARNHAM

GUILDFORD

DORKING

REIGATE

CRAWLEY

WEST
SUSSEX

HORSHAM

PETERSFIELD

MIDHURST

PETWORTH

R. ARUN

PORTSMOUTH

CHICHESTER

ARUNDEL

BRIGHTON

WORTHING

BOGNOR REGIS

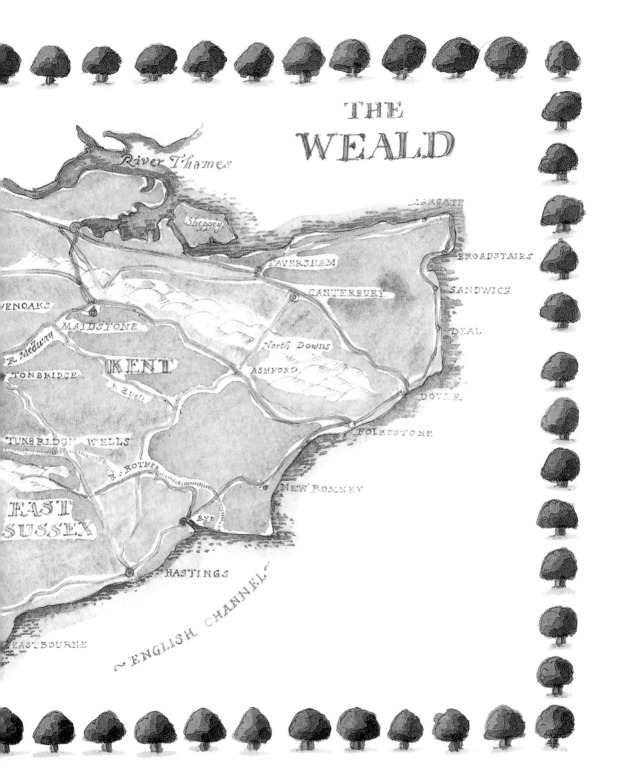

THE
WEALD

River Thames

Sheppey

MARGATE

FAVERSHAM

BROADSTAIRS

CANTERBURY

SANDWICH

ENOAKS

DEAL

MAIDSTONE

R. Medway

North Downs

KENT

ASHFORD

TONBRIDGE

R. Bult

DOVER

FOLKESTONE

TUNBRIDGE WELLS

R. ROTHER

NEW ROMNEY

EAST
SUSSEX

RYE

HASTINGS

~ENGLISH CHANNEL~

EASTBOURNE

The WEALD

IN ANCIENT times, woods of oak, ash and elm covered south-east England. From Kent, through what is now Sussex, to the edge of Hampshire the forest of the Weald grew on the clay-bearing ground between the two ranges of chalk hills that form the North and South Downs. The oak trees which provided the timbers for the ships of the British navy also gave rise to the Wealden half-timbered house like the farmhouse near Billinghurst illustrated overleaf.

Here, the oak and the clay in which it grew are combined in one of the most pleasing of vernacular house types. While becoming more sophisticated over the centuries, the basic plan of the houses remained the same—they were laid out in a rectangle, with a large double-height central hall and a projecting upper storey. Although these houses are now often concealed behind facades of brick or rendering, the original form still shows.

During the late middle ages the forest was gradually felled to provide fuel for the iron-smelting industry which at that time was centered in Sussex. As the supply of timber dwindled, clay became the more dominant building material both as bricks and as tiles, the latter used not only for roofing but also hung as an external cladding on a timber-framed structure. This tile hanging is a particular feature of the Weald and it can be extremely decorative when used in repeating patterns, examples of which are shown at Northchapel and in the granary at Peper Harow.

A horseshoe-shaped seam of chalk runs from the Dorset coast through Hampshire branching to meet the sea in two directions, to the north along the southern side of the Thames basin and to the south through the Downs to the English Channel. As a building material this principally manifests itself as flint. A very durable stone, found in rather small pieces which can not be cut, flint is unsuitable for structural work on its own and must be contained between brick edging or used in conjunction with blocks of solid chalk.

The contrast between the deep blue of the flint's centre with its white chalk surrounding produces a wonderful texture in the predominant construction method of the downland villages from Hampshire to Kent. The house in Wisborough Green is brick and flint, subsequently painted white. The only other stone found is a sandstone that runs along the north of the Downs and is visible in towns like Midhurst and Petworth, and also used primarily in conjunction with brick quoins and for door and window surrounds.

Further east weather-boarding is used as cladding, made either from durable elm or from imported Scandinavian pine, as seen in the houses at Folkestone, Ashford and Sandwich. Among the most remarkable vernacular building types of the area are the net-drying sheds in Hastings (shown overleaf), a good example of fitness to purpose as no other use would require such tall structures. They are unique to this part of the south coast, their function dictating their form and giving evidence of the everyday history and concerns of the region.

SOUTH HARTING ·WEST SUSSEX·

Nr ASHFORD · KENT

Granite and slate are the only building materials not found in the Weald. Timber, brick, tiles, chalk, flints and sandstone are all used in different parts of the region.

Particularly satisfactory combinations of these are found at Witley, where chips of black flint have been stuck into the mortar between blocks of chalk, and in the chequerboard pattern of flints and chalk blocks at Canterbury shown overleaf.

Much of the beauty of the Wealden villages lies in the colour of the brick, which varies from deep red to warm apricot and from bluish grey to the hideous Midhurst white. Sadly these regional variations are fast disappearing as standardization means that the same brick is made in Lewes and Liverpool, scientifically prepared to the same perfect formula (which, mysteriously, seems often prone to unsightly 'sweating'!). It is in this way that we lose our architectural heritage. The door in Petworth is remarkable in being so tall and thin. It is part of a terrace in which each house has the same rather economical frontage.

Nr BILLINGSHURST · EAST SUSSEX

FOLKESTONE
KENT

HASTINGS
EAST · SUSSEX

SOUTH HARTING
WEST SUSSEX

NORTHCHAPEL
WEST SUSSEX

WISBOROUGH GREEN
WEST SUSSEX

SINGLETON
WEST SUSSEX

Nr SANDWICH
KENT

PEPER HAROW
SURREY

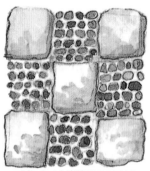

N\. CANTERBURY
KENT

WITLEY
SURREY

NORTHCHAPEL
WEST SUSSEX

PETWORTH WEST SUSSEX

SOUTH HARTING
WEST SUSSEX

WESTWELL
KENT

Nʀ LEWES
EAST SUSSEX

WITLEY
SURREY

SINGLETON
WEST · SUSSEX

SMARDEN
KENT

SINGLETON
WEST SUSSEX

A THATCHED COTTAGE
in SINGLETON

IN the Downs that run from Hampshire and Dorset through Sussex to the Brighton coast chalk is the principle building material. It is often used in combination with flint, its natural partner in the distinctive geological formation that shapes the local landscape.

This cottage at Singleton in West Sussex is made of irregular blocks of chalk and flint with quoins, lintels and edgings of brick. The roof is steeply pitched and deep eaves overhang the house so that the rain runs off quickly without damaging the chalk walls or allowing the thatch to become damp.

Thatch has several obvious advantages as a roofing material: it is cool in summer and warm in winter. It is extremely light and is almost soundproof. In the days when wheat was harvested by hand, it was the cheapest roofing available. However, combine harvesters bruise the stalks and the modern varieties

of wheat grown commercially have such short stalks that thatching with them is impossible. Good quality materials have become much harder to obtain and hence more expensive. But there is hope, demand is growing and so thatching straw may become more available.

The thatch is laid on top of thin battens attached to the rafters. The thatcher starts at the eaves and lays small flat bundles, called yealms, in overlapping courses. The way the thatch is shaped over the dormer windows and gables and the type of ornamentation on the ridge distinguishes the work of one thatcher from another.

A wheat-straw roof, like this one, might last thirty years while one made of reed, which is common in East Anglia and in parts of Dorset and Hampshire, is more durable and will only need to be renewed in seventy five to a hundred years if the householder is lucky.

SINGLETON WEST SUSSEX

EAST ANGLIA

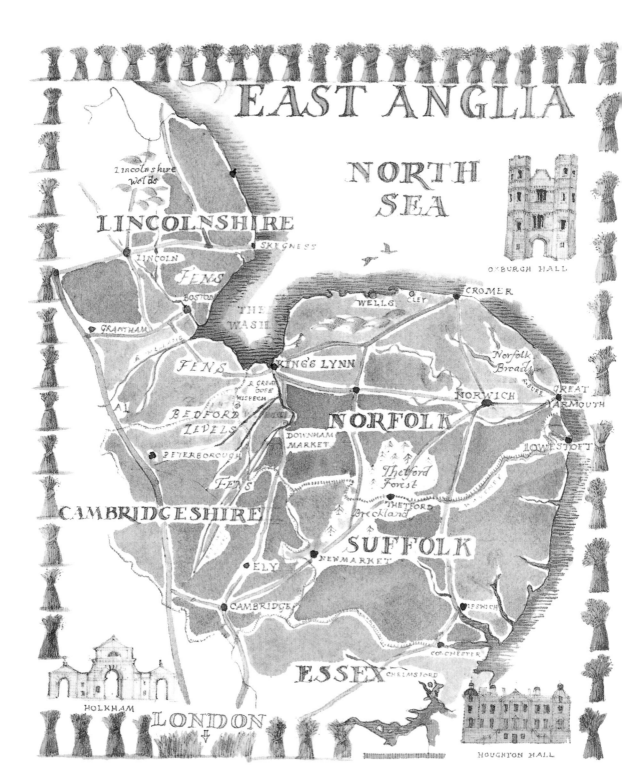

EAST ANGLIA

EAST ANGLIA owes its preservation to being on the way to nowhere. Until recently it was badly served by trunk roads and motorways and it has remained comparatively unspoilt by development. Its flat or gently rolling countryside is one of Britain's most intensively farmed regions. Known as the bread basket of England, East Anglia is now arable country and consists of large fields of wheat and barley, interspersed with sugar beet, which stretch to the horizon. You can drive for miles without seeing a cow. Although once an area of rich mixed farming, it was the growing of crops that gave rise to the splendid barns and farmyards.

The dramatic low-lying fens which stretch north from the cathedral town of Ely to The Wash, were peat bogs until drained in the eighteenth century and turned into rich farmland. The region is surrounded on three sides by the sea and on the coast are the fishing villages and harbours that continue the centuries-old trade with continental Europe through the ports of Holland and Germany. The very coastline is always changing; the old Suffolk town of Dunwich has almost all fallen into the sea as the low sandy cliffs on which it stands have been eroded by the waves. While on the north Norfolk coast the villages surrounding the River Glaven—Cley, Glandford, Wiveton and Blake-ney—were once all bustling ports. Now they are stranded with no water as, due to silting and shifting sand bars and spits, the harbour basin has been reduced to a small river flowing through meadows. Only the elaborate medieval churches and fine merchants' houses of these now unassuming villages reveal their former wealth.

Wide seams of clay underlie the region and the resulting soft, red bricks are typically laid in elaborate patterns. In Cambridgeshire and West Norfolk a yellow clay is found which is made into an unattractive brick but, mixed with straw and moulded into blocks, it produces a durable building material called cob which is used unfired then rendered for protection against the weather. In the southern part of Suffolk and in Essex and Cambridgeshire, external plasterwork is often formed into delicate and often representational patterns, a craft unique to the area, known as pargetting.

Flint is the most common building stone and is used layered in courses, arranged in chequerboard patterns with other materials or randomly mixed with broken bricks or rubble and often contained by brick quoining. Another local stone is brown carstone quarried along the north coast and evident in villages east of Kings Lynn. Carstone is usually used in pieces no larger than a pear.

SANDRINGHAM
NORFOLK

SAFFRON WALDEN
ESSEX

STRATFORD St MARY · SUFFOLK

SHIPDHAM · NORFOLK.

Nr AUDLEY END · ESSEX

Nr BURY St EDMUNDS   SUFFOLK

Nʀ ELY · CAMBRIDGESHIRE

ELY

BRANCASTER   NORFOLK

FAKENHAM

GLANDFORD · NORFOLK

CLEY · NORFOLK

MORSTON   NORFOLK

BURNHAM NORTON · NORFOLK

NR CROMER
NORFOLK

CLEY
NORFOLK

NR LOUTH
LINCOLNSHIRE

NR SKEGNESS
LINCOLNSHIRE

HEYDON · NORFOLK

NR BECCLES
SUFFOLK

BRAINTREE
ESSEX

CASTLE ACRE
NORFOLK

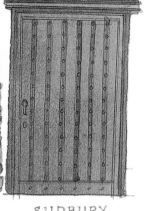

SUDBURY
SUFFOLK

BRANCASTER
NORFOLK

HEYDON · NORFOLK

E AST Anglian buildings are rich in textural qualities. Chalk blocks are laid with knapped flint in checkerboard patterns, flint pebbles are carefully sized and laid in rows, and chalk stone is used in small, uneven blocks with flint and bricks. Lintels and facings may be made of the local brick to give strength to walls of knapped flints. The decorative brick-work for which East Anglia is famous includes delicate edgings and moulded bricks for the curved Dutch gables and patterned chimney stacks. An unusual regional feature is the cross-over brick lintel, which is found from Norfolk through Lincolnshire to Yorkshire. Thatch is still used for roofing, but the dominant mate-rial is pantile.

BURNHAM NORTON · NORFOLK

A FARMHOUSE
near
BURNHAM MARKET

A typical example of its kind, this Norfolk farmhouse is built of a soft, red brick, sometimes interspersed with blue. The three-bay facade is given incident by the string course that divides the ground and first floors and by the extended brick lintel above the ground floor windows. The rear and end elevations show the building to be principally constructed of flint, chalk and brick used as rubble stone with brick quoining and lintels.

Careful observation of local features characterizes the renovation of this house. The pattern made by the brickwork where the eaves meet the wall to the left of the French windows; the particularly pleasing composition of chalk and brick in the gable-end of the attached barn; the characteristic long roof of the dormer window at the rear of the kitchen block; the use of large pantiles as a roofing material—all these are well-considered, locally authentic, and combine to extremely good effect.

This is a particularly good example of sensitive restoration, although major changes have taken place. New window frames have replaced decayed older ones; new openings have been pierced in walls; a new dormer window has been inserted and the lean-to behind the kitchen has been completely rebuilt. Yet sympathetic attention to detail has made positive assets of all these changes. The builders have been responsive to the need to preserve rather than replace and the owners clearly have a thorough understanding of those qualities and features that must be retained. It would have been so easy to use unsuitable doors and windows, to render the rear elevation or to point it incorrectly.

The final appearance will rely on careful planting of the garden. In this case, the proposed low box hedges around beds of cottage flowers, a mixed orchard and a row of pleached limes along the road boundary will complete the felicitous effect and make this once-derelict property into a pretty village house, well-integrated into its surroundings while responding imaginatively to the living requirements of its owners.

GATTON THORPE

NORFOLK CHURCHES

IN the middle ages East Anglia was the most densely populated area in Britain and at that time there were at least one hundred and fifty more villages than there are now. Each village was grouped around a church and many of these churches survive, sometimes alone and ghostly in a field of sugar beet, the last vestige of a lost community. Church towers are a prominent feature of the Norfolk landscape; as much a part of the character of the region as are Wren's spires in the City of London.

The earliest buildings, like those at Gatton Thorpe and Worthing, have squat round towers, a convenient and inexpensive shape to build as, having no corners, indigenous flint could be used on its own without recourse to more expensive brick or imported cut stone. From impressive Norman structures, such as South Lopham, the churches of East Anglia become increasingly more elaborate with time, culminating in Decorated buildings like St Mary's at Cley. This fine church, built to serve a bustling port, was conceived on the grandest scale and would have been grander still had not the silting up of the river Glaven and the later decline of the town called a halt to its expansion.

SOUTH LOPHAM

HALES · SUFFOLK

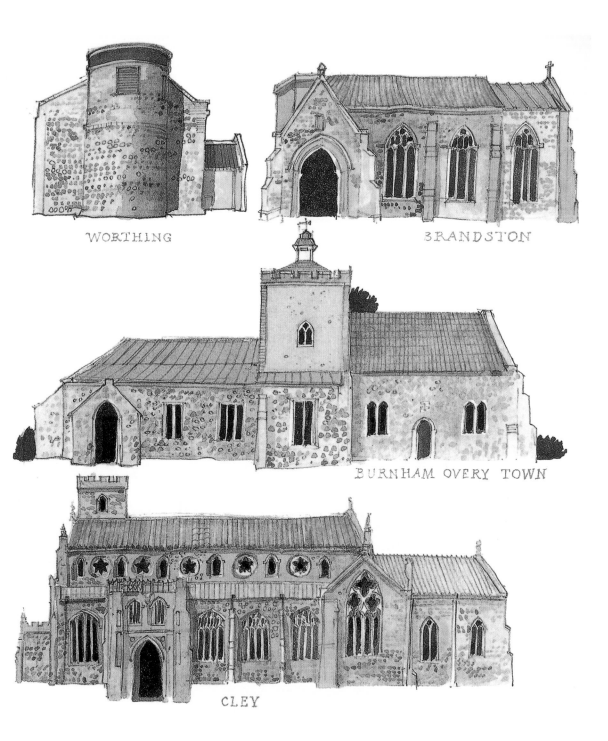

WORTHING

BRANDSTON

BURNHAM OVERY TOWN

CLEY

CLEY & WIVETON · NORFOLK

The SHIRES

The SHIRES

THE SHIRES lie at the heart of England. From the rich farmland of Buckinghamshire and Bedfordshire, through Northamptonshire to the countries of Leicestershire and Nottinghamshire, the landscape consists principally of gently rolling grassland. The countryside is divided by thick-laid hedges, impressive reminders of an age-old craft that, with the advent of the modern mechanical flail, has all but disappeared elsewhere in the country. The preservation of hedges in the Shires is testament to the strong tradition of foxhunting in the area and its enthusiastic support by local farmers and landowners. This is the home of the Quorn, the Pytchley and the Belvoir, the most famous packs of foxhounds in the world.

This central part of Britain is badly afflicted by motorways and roads, the M1 and A1 slice through it, dividing the area into three. Perhaps because of this there remain very remote-seeming parts only a mile or two from heavy traffic.

The Romans built Leicester using large quantities of broad, flat, tile-like bricks fired from local clays, but it is only since the middle of the nineteenth century that this material has come into extensive use again. Brick predominates in the central and western part of the region, and, to a lesser extent, half-timbered construction, often with brick infill, called nogging. Typically, buildings are straight-fronted and plain; indeed this is probably one of the least ornamental areas in the country. Such elaboration as there is usually consists of decorative brick infill in half-timbered buildings or features, such as string courses and mouldings, built as an integral part of brickwork construction.

In the eastern part of the Shires, stone becomes available and entire villages are built of the orange, red and golden-brown ironstones, also known as marlstones, which are contained in the limestone belt that continues from the Cotswolds through the east of the region. In Buckinghamshire and Bedfordshire the limestone is an inferior type of oolite which tends to crumble and, for this reason, many of the buildings are rendered in rough cast for protection against the weather. The limestones found in the northern part of Northamptonshire, around Stamford, rank among the very best of the oolites to be found in Britain. Not only are they very finely textured, but they are more frost-resistant than the Cotswold variety. Although they do not cover such an extensive area, the oolite villages of Northamptonshire are as inherently beautiful as those of the Cotswolds, sharing the delicacy of the carved and ashlared detailing and the contrast of smooth surfaces against rough.

BILSTONE · LEICESTER

REDMILE · LEICESTERSHIRE

Nʀ EASTWELL. LEICESTERSHIRE

BARKESTONE·LE·VALE

NEAR NOTTINGHAM

Nʀ SHELTON·NOTTS

PEACOCK INN

Nʀ MARKET HARBOROUGH

Nʀ COTON. NORTHAMPTONSHIRE

Nᵣ OAKHAM LEICESTERSHIRE

In the Shires the roofs are more varied than in any other region as shown in the examples on the previous page. Thatch is quite common, particularly on half-timbered and brick houses, or with limestone, as on the cottage near Eastwell, Leicestershire. The two roofing materials most associated with the region are pantiles and slate. The subtle colouring of the slate goes well with the soft, red brick of the graceful three-storeyed barn near Coton in Northamptonshire; the colours of the slate range from blue-grey to a pinkish-purple.

Pantiles are Dutch in origin but have been manufactured in Britain since the eighteenth century. Roof shapes are kept simple, like those of the houses just outside Nottingham and at Shelton, because the size and shape of the pantiles make it awkward to incorporate valleys and dormers. Usually warm red, pantiles are also seen in grey, although these are usually of more recent manufacture. An example of this is the pub near Market Harborough.

The prevalence of large quantities of good building stone in the Shires is obvious from the widespread stone detailing, such as that round the windows of the Eastwell church or in the wide ashlared door surround and drip-lintel in the building in the centre of the opposite page. Where the stone is of a poorer quality, brick is often used to edge the door and window openings, as in the stable door at Shelton.

Interesting minor details abound, such as the elegant iron railings from near Corby, or the simple, yet charming, timber garden gate near Ravensthorpe.

NEAR RAVENSTHORPE
NORTHAMPTONSHIRE

EASTWELL

BARKESTONE ʟᵉ VALE.
LEICESTERSHIRE

Nᵒˢ COTTESBROKE

SHELTON · NOTTS

Nᴿ CORBY
NORTHAMPTONSHIRE

EASTWELL LEICESTERSHIRE

A COTTAGE in BILSTONE

Bᴏᴛʜ halves of this Leicestershire cottage would originally have been built of brick but the right-hand side has since been rendered, added character being provided by the exposed wooden lintels above the windows. Now the cottages are linked by a common roof and it is this roof that is particularly remarkable. Corrugated iron has been laid over thatch following the contours of the roof and the dormer windows. The exposed ends of the straw are protected by weather boarding. This is an unusual use of a much-maligned building material which is more commonly associated with temporary structures. It forms a patina which blends in extremely well with the landscape and is particularly pleasing when covered with many coats of black bitumastic paint. It is a popular misconception that every green blends well with the countryside, but the green of paint is different from that of grass or foliage while black, being a neutral colour and not competing with nature, makes a safer bet.

Housing in a village is at a premium and, due to the virtual demise of rented property, it is now almost impossible for newly married couples to find accommodation in the villages in which they grew up. New buildings should be possible in all villages and should enhance, not damage, their appearance.

In the 1950s and 1960s the majority of new estates were built in a style that has no vernacular precedents. The houses in Corby are examples of this; built of a characterless brick in the middle of a stone-built town, metal windows and debased classical porches sit beneath an unbroken roofline. More recently, an increased interest in traditional buildings has encouraged the developer to adopt a faux vernacular facing as in the first floor of the house in Malton. However, half-timbering is not a building style found in North Yorkshire

LONGNOR · North Staffordshire

Nr CORBY
NORTHAMPTONSHIRE

nor are the leaded panes or treacly stained garage doors typical.

The house in Longnor, on the other hand, does reflect the vernacular of North Staffordshire and Derbyshire. Although in no way a reproduction, the use of simple stone mouldings around the doors and windows and the breaking of the roofline with chimneys make this a most successful essay in the local style.

The two maps below illustrate one of the major faults in planning regulations. So great is the obsession with the car that in plan A, where the suggested need for off-street parking and garaging is met, only six houses can fit into the area that in plan B accommodates ten. The use of a car park releases ground for a central green where children can play. Plan B also allows for more contact with neighbours as the houses are not isolated from each other.

Nᴿ MALTON
YORKSHIRE

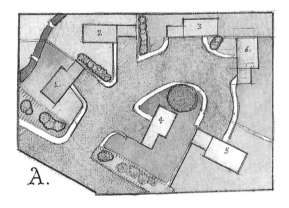

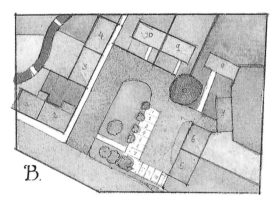

The COTSWOLDS

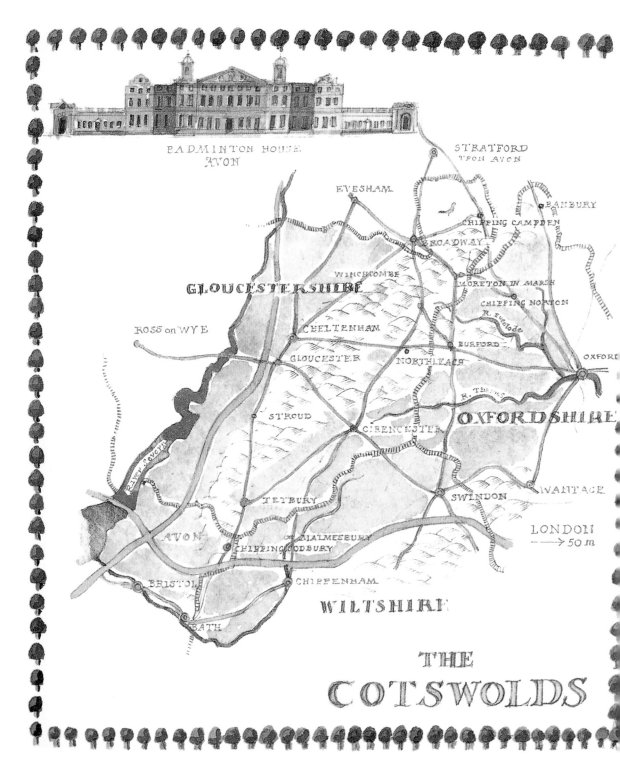

BADMINTON HOUSE
AVON

STRATFORD
UPON AVON

EVESHAM

BANBURY

CHIPPING CAMPDEN

BROADWAY

WINCHCOMBE

GLOUCESTERSHIRE

MORETON IN MARSH

CHIPPING NORTON

R. Evenlode

ROSS on WYE

CHELTENHAM

BURFORD

GLOUCESTER

NORTHLEACH

OXFORD

R. Thames

STROUD

CIRENCESTER

OXFORDSHIRE

River Severn

WANTAGE

TETBURY

SWINDON

AVON

MALMESBURY

CHIPPING SODBURY

LONDON
→ 50 m

BRISTOL

CHIPPENHAM

WILTSHIRE

BATH

THE
COTSWOLDS

The COTSWOLDS

ALL THE buildings in the Cotswolds look alike in one way as, from the manor house to the smallest cottage, every house is an exercise in the same style. This style is a legacy from the sixteenth century—of heavily mullioned windows, drip-mouldings where the protruding line of the masonry above the windows drops down through a right angle taking the water away from the walls, and dormer windows poking out of heavy stone roofs. Most extraordinary though is the stone. The warm yellow limestone, oolite, is part of the limestone belt that runs from the Dorset to the Yorkshire coast and is at its widest in the Cotswolds.

There are huge quantities of limestone only just below the surface throughout the area. So easily accessible is it, that every wall and garden shed has been built from Cotswold stone, giving the Cotswolds more perfect villages per square mile than anywhere else in Britain. Oolite is easily workable when quarried but hardens with exposure to the atmosphere. This has led to a very high standard of decorative masonry, particularly in the splendid town and village churches.

If Chipping Camden is the most northerly point, then a line taken via Broadway, Malmesbury, Swindon, Oxford and through Chipping Norton back to Camden would enclose the Cotswolds proper, but the building style continues south to Bath and north towards Bicester. Towns, such as Burford, Camden, Bourton-on-the-Water and Cirencester, all have quite unfair proportions of perfect town houses with squat gothic doors or grander, classical porches and lichen-covered stone roofs sagging worryingly under their own weight. There are also the villages of Dyrham, Lacock and Little Barrington which are entirely faultless and unspoilt.

The medieval wealth of the Cotswolds was due principally to wool. The powerful ecclesiastical and secular landlords cleared and enclosed large areas—evicting and demolishing whole villages to create bigger and more profitable sheep walks. So profitable was the wool trade, that it became almost an embarrassment to some in the monastic establishments who tried to curb the financial acumen of their abbots. A weaving industry grew up alongside and the area remained extremely prosperous until the Industrial Revolution, when cloth manufacture moved north to Lancashire and cotton imports began to increase. It was the ensuing depression in the late eighteenth and nineteenth centuries that ensured the preservation of many Cotswold buildings.

More recently, the beauty of the area, coupled with royal patronage and relative closeness to London, has brought about development, conversion and renovation. This trio is having a fatal effect on the area; new houses are built of bland reconstituted stone—which does not have the subtle colour variations and liveliness of the native limestone—and, as the population of these villages changes from farm worker to computer worker, the kind of gentrification now so prevalent in our villages blunders on, oblivious to the traditions of the area.

CROPREDY OXFORDSHIRE

SNOWSHILL
GLOUCESTERSHIRE

LACOCK · WILTSHIRE

BURFORD

BURFORD
OXFORDSHIRE

LACOCK
WILTSHIRE

GREAT TEW
OXFORDSHIRE

Nʳ CIRENCESTER
GLOUCESTERSHIRE

GREAT TEW
OXFORDSHIRE

DAGLINGWORTH
GLOUCESTERSHIRE

MUCH of the beauty of the Cotswolds' buildings is derived from the subtle balance between the often elaborately carved mouldings and blocks of undressed stone. Failure to recognize and imitate this balance in new buildings and on extensions to old houses creates a discordant note.

The door surround and pediment on the Rissington house and porch at Filkins are fine examples of stonecarving, but the stone mason really comes into his own when more elaborate detailing is required—such as the scrolls on the Mickleton pediment, the urn and bracket at Lacock, or the return label mould above the window at Burford.

DORMER WINDOW
Farringdon

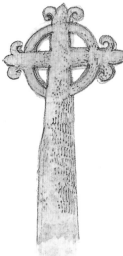

CROSS

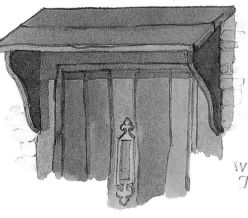

PORCH *Barrington*

PORCH
Filkins

WINDOW
Tew

DOOR · *Rissington*

WINDOW *Burford*

BRACKET LACOCK

DORMER WINDOW *Castle Combe*

URN *Lacock*

WINDOW *Lacock*

DOOR *Mickleton*

A HOUSE
in GREAT TEW

T HE natural advantage of an area such as the Cotswolds—its ample supplies of a building stone that can be easily worked and used not only for the body of the building, but for the detailing and for the roof—creates immensely appealing buildings such as this one in Great Tew.

The house has been added to at various times over the years. Rather than destroying the simple balance of the original composition, each addition seems to have enhanced the building. The fact that the same building material is used obviously helps but, equally important, is the way the natural edges of the central building have been extended by echoing its original proportions and elevations. Another factor is the uniformity of style. Although the windows are of different sizes, they are edged with stone mullions in the Cotswold manner. The most unusual feature is the wooden doorway and even that, with its decorative tracery, is distinctly of the region.

SIDE ELEVATION

SIDE ELEVATION

SIDE WINDOW

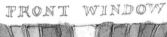

FRONT WINDOW

SIDE DOOR

A.

B.

A COTSWOLD BARN CONVERSION

THE Cotswolds contain some of the finest traditional barns in Britain but, as modern farming techniques have different requirements of their buildings, they have outlived their working life. Barns have proved an irresistible temptation to farmers and developers who found in the late 1980s that these redundant buildings were worth more than the rest of their land.

The countryside is scarred with the results of the work of these speculators. All too often, as in the example below left, the stone roof is pierced with shining skylights, the architectural form of the doorway is broken up—in this case with a wildly out-of-context 'Georgian-style' door—and an unsuitable feature, such as this 'Victorian-style' conservatory is added. The new windows, with which the walls are dotted, are in a style with no architectural antecedents and stained a particularly nasty treacly brown, much favoured in new developments.

By demolishing the lean-tos and altering the overall shape of the building, much of the character of this barn has been lost while charmless fencing and straight-edged driveways and walks have suburbanized the yard. A car stands proudly and all-too-visibly in its horrid car port.

In theory the conversion shown below is a better one but, although there are fewer architectural incursions—the outbuildings have been kept and the grounds are less manicured—the appearance of the barn has been altered to such an extent that its original purpose as a farm building has been lost. Rather than becoming a country house, it is now an awkward hybrid.

Barns are as important to the look of the English countryside as churches and houses, punctuating the fields and hedges. We are historically an agricultural population and these buildings are its monuments and should be preserved as such.

FARMINGTON *gloucestershire*

The WEST MIDLANDS

THE WEST MIDLANDS

CHESHIRE

STOKE ON TRENT

UTTOXETER

OSWESTRY

ECCLESHALL

STAFFORD

BURTON ON TRENT

R. TRENT

NEWPORT

SHREWSBURY

STAFFORDSHIRE

TELFORD

LICHFIELD

WOLVERHAMPTON

SHROPSHIRE

BIRMINGHAM

KIDDERMINSTER

COVENTRY

LUDLOW

R. TEME

LEOMINSTER

WARWICK

STRATFORD UPON AVON

HEREFORD
and
WORCESTER

WORCESTER

HEREFORDSHIRE

MALVERN

R. AVON

EVESHAM

TEWKESBURY

GLOUCESTERSHIRE

ROSS ON WYE

GLOUCESTER

R. SEVERN

The WEST MIDLANDS

FROM STRATFORD-UPON-AVON north through the West Midlands there is a narrow seam of clay from which bricks are made. The distinctive red of these bricks becomes more intense the further north you go, until they meet the red sandstone of Cheshire. Brick buildings with their thatched or tiled roofs look particularly fine against the reddish earth and greenness of the Marches landscape. Apart from the city of Birmingham and the industrial towns that grew up around it in the nineteenth century, the region has always been slightly removed from the centres of money and power and much of it has not been tampered with. Architecturally, the West Midlands are unique: not for brick or stone building, but rather because in this thin stretch of land are concentrated more half-timbered buildings than anywhere else in Britain. Indeed, Worcestershire, Herefordshire and to a lesser extent Shropshire are often referred to as the black-and-white counties after the characteristic timber-framed buildings.

There are three principal building methods. The earliest, and most distinctive, is the cruck method. If the structural timbers in a cruck house have not been covered over it is possible to see how similar its construction is, albeit inverted, to that of a wooden sailing ship. Two timbers, often mirror images as they are two halves of the same tree trunk, are leant one against the other at either end of the building. From the outside, the other two methods appear much the same, but in one, the box-frame, the side walls are load bearing while in the other, called post-and-truss and similar in some ways to cruck construction, the weight of the roof is conveyed by a series of vertical frames ranged along the building at intervals. Pale imitations of these techniques are cynically attached to so many modern houses, adding a superficial character while showing a failure to understand the original purpose of the timbers. In the last ten years a renewed interest in timber-framed buildings has resulted in many buildings being dismantled, every member carefully numbered, then re-erected elsewhere, sometimes in America or even Japan.

All these construction methods are found throughout Britain but are predominant in the West Midlands where the builders have added their own decorative touches, such as rows of ornamental panels incorporated into the facades of many of the grander half-timbered houses. Perhaps the most famous of these is Little Moreton Hall, a property in the care of the National Trust.

Sadly, the skills involved in building timber frames from scratch make it so prohibitively expensive that this is not really a living tradition. Consequently, sensitive repair and restoration is even more important and a thorough knowledge even more vital.

IN cruck construction, pairs of curving members, sometimes split vertically from the same tree trunk, are set into the ground at intervals along the building and tied at the top, or ridge, to form triangular frames. These are then joined by purlins over which are laid rafters. In the cottage at Weobley, the horizontal tie beams have made it possible to create another storey and to allow for a vertically-sided lower area. The Cropthorne cottage and the two-storey dovecot at Luntley Court, Herefordshire, are typical of post-and-truss construction in which the weight of the building is carried on a series of frames identical to the ones revealed on the gable end.

The scale of the dovecote at Luntley Court may surprise present-day viewers, used to thinking of this type of building as a charming, if anachronistic, feature of many farmyards and manor houses. But dovecotes were, until the eighteenth century, an important part of the rural economy. A valuable source of winter meat, pigeons were kept in large numbers. A building such as this one would have housed two hundred pairs of birds. These birds were often a bone of contention between their owner, usually the Lord of the Manor, and neighbouring farmers and villagers, as they were allowed to fly freely, to the considerable detriment of crops.

With the coming of the agricultural revolution and, particularly, the introduction of the turnip as winter fodder, animals could be over-wintered for the first time and, thereafter, replaced squab (young pigeon) as the principal source of fresh meat. Today, dovecotes remain as relics of an earlier agricultural system, often housing a purely decorative flock of fantail pigeons no longer destined for the pot.

WEOBLEY
HEREFORDSHIRE

DOVECOT · LUNTLEY COURT
HEREFORDSHIRE

PEMBRIDGE
HEREFORDSHIRE

WEOBLEY
HEREFORDSHIRE

CROPTHORNE
WORCESTERSHIRE

Nʳ LUDLOW · SHROPSHIRE

O NE of the attractions of thatch is that it can be easily shaped to curve over windows, as in the half-timbered house near Ludlow, shown on the previous page. Or it can follow idiosyncratic designs such as that of the cottages at Frampton-upon-Severn in Gloucestershire in which the roofing material has been swept low in exaggerated loops. Flat clay tiles are the roofing material on the house at Pembridge and the Luntley Court dovecote on the previous page, but in the stone building in Shropshire the same material is carried through to the roof.

The West Midlands is renowned for the decorative panelling that is often incorporated into the half-timbering. Gnarled or twisted branches of oak, or carved pieces of timber, were used to form patterns including diamonds, triangles, quatrefoils, herringbones and stars, as shown in the typical examples opposite. The repetition of these patterns in adjacent framed panels not only enhanced the overall decorative effect, but allowed considerable scope for the individual craftsman to stamp his own personality on the building.

FRAMPTON · UPON · SEVERN
GLOUCESTERSHIRE

Nᴿ BRIDGENORTH
SHROPSHIRE

PEMBRIDGE · HEREFORDSHIRE

NANTWICH   CHESHIRE

STOKESAY CASTLE · SHROPSHIRE

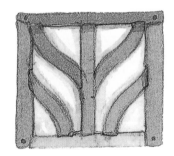

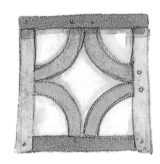

A HOUSE in BROMYARD

THE grand scale of this square-framed Herefordshire yeoman's farmhouse, which is well over three hundred years old, gives some idea of the wealth and standing of its original owner who would have seen the building as a deliberate expression of status. Built on a sloping site, the deep plinth of stone provides a dry foundation as well as a level base. The steep pitch of the tiled roof indicates that Tower Hill House was probably thatched when first built—almost certainly, the two gabled windows were added later. The detailing is simple lattice windows of small glazed panes set into wooden mullions, the two-storey gabled entranceway has a plank door and the simple-but-decorative panelling is made up of diamonds with a more elaborate quatrefoil on the side elevation.

In the strength and firmness of its dramatically displayed structure, with each element playing a true part in the construction, this farmhouse is a splendid example of the 'real thing' and such a far cry from the ignorantly applied, purely decorative timbering so beloved of modern speculative developers.

ARDELEY HERTFORDSHIRE

Nr HEYDON · NORFOLK

BLAISE HAMLET · AVON

PORT SUNLIGHT
MERSEYSIDE

MODEL VILLAGES

N.ᴿ BRIDGEWATER
SOMERSET

NEWBURY
BERKSHIRE

THE passion with which the landowners of the late eighteenth century embraced the agricultural revolution and the revival of interest in farming among the upper classes coincided with increasing alarm at the fate of their neighbours across the Channel during the French revolution and a genuine concern sparked by reformers like Cobbett. This fertile combination of self-interest and philanthropy led to reform of the squalid conditions in which the English labourer then lived.

Milton Abbas in Dorset was amongst the first of a series of model villages which combined social conscience with a less admirable desire to sanitize and prettify the cottages of the farm worker. This vogue for the picturesque produced the beautiful but idealized version of the cottage, the 'cottage ornée', most famous and emulated of which was Nash's Blaise Hamlet near Bristol. A simpler, but no less-pleasing style was employed at Heydon in Norfolk. The Pump House at Ardeley is an Edwardian improvement to a model village, while Port Sunlight in Merseyside was an attempt by Lord Leverhulme to create a perfect environment for the industrial labourer and was the precursor of the garden-suburb movement of this century.

HEYDON NORFOLK

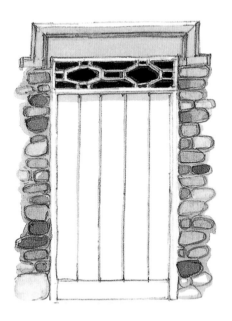

WALES

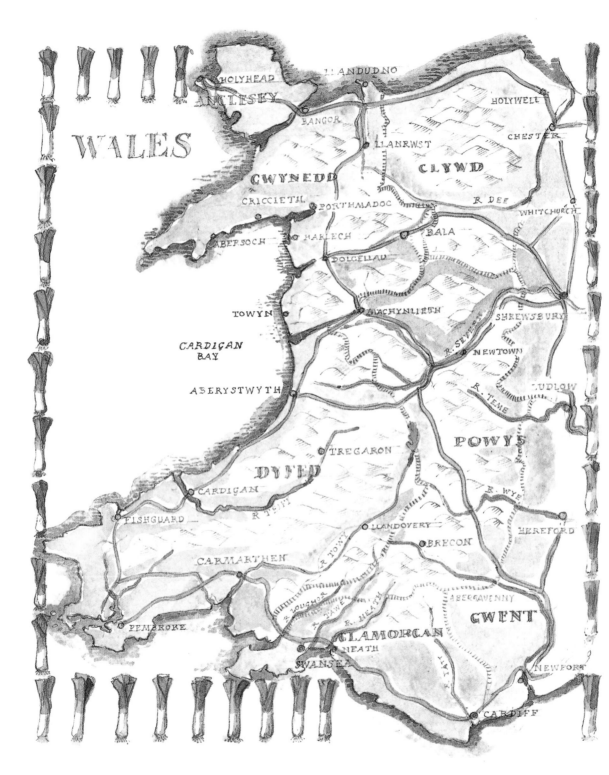

WALES

_ALTHOUGH FIERCELY independent and craving devolution from Westminster, Wales is an intrinsic part of Britain. There is no dramatic change in landscape or buildings as you cross the border, a border which only manifests itself by the appearance of consonant-ridden Welsh place names.

Although lowland areas exist in Glamorgan, Gwent and Pembroke, the Welsh landscape is largely mountainous. The deep wooded valleys north of Swansea lead inland through the once-famous Welsh coalfields. Here a striking contrast between factory, town and wilderness provides the dominant character. Around Merthyr Tydfil and Aberdare terraces of labourers' cottages fill the valleys but stop abruptly as bracken and heather cover the ridges before swooping down into another industrial centre. Along the bosky border with England, the half-timbered buildings of Hereford and Worcester continue into Powys. As the ground becomes more hilly so stone becomes the more prevalent building material. The Cambrian mountains, Snowdonia, the Black Mountains and the beautiful Brecon Beacons, compose the centre of Wales; from their sources here the rivers Wye and Severn flow on to become one of Britain's three great river systems. In this wild and wet part of the country the architecture is bleak and devoid of frills, plain simplicity giving charm to some buildings while the dead grey granite lends austere beauty to the mountain villages.

Further north, the mountains of Clwyd are heather topped and the valleys sustain a richer form of agriculture. Here, more substantial houses spread eastwards towards Cheshire. This north-eastern section has traditionally been most closely aligned with England. Fine towns like Ruthin show a degree of prosperity lacking elsewhere.

Perhaps the most beautiful buildings of Wales are to be found along its coast. From Pembrokeshire, where the architecture is reminiscent of Devon, the broad sweep of Cardigan Bay contains the near-perfect seaside town of Aberdyfi, while an architectural curiosity is to be found at Port Merion, near Porth Madog. Here in the 1920s the architect Clough Williams-Ellis designed an artists' colony. This village looking over beautiful Tremadoc Bay, is built not in the Welsh vernacular but in that of the Italian Riviera. Tuscan belvederes and shuttered, stuccoed Mediterranean facades cluster around a square. Although now rather shabby and forlorn, it retains its rather fey charm and melancholy beauty. Rolling green country continues through Criccieth to the port of Abersoch where whitewashed stone cottages tumble down to the sea.

In the 1970s the low prices of Welsh property led to a sharp increase in the proportion of houses being used as second homes. The unfriendly and arsonist tendencies of various nationalist Welsh organisations, who set fire to many such holiday cottages, has stemmed this tide and has been successful in keeping Welsh prices well below their English counterparts.

RUTHIN · CLYWD

FAIRBOURNE
GWYNEDD

Nʳ NEWPORT · GWENT

RUTHIN
CLYWD

Nʳ DOLGELLAU
GWYNEDD

NEATH · GLAMORGAN

N' DOLGELLAU

N' MOLD
CLYWD

LLIDIARDAU · GWYNEDD

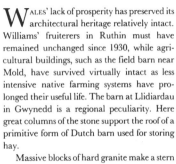

WALES' lack of prosperity has preserved its architectural heritage relatively intact. Williams' fruiterers in Ruthin must have remained unchanged since 1930, while agricultural buildings, such as the field barn near Mold, have survived virtually intact as less intensive native farming systems have prolonged their useful life. The barn at Llidiardau in Gwynedd is a regional peculiarity. Here great columns of the stone support the roof of a primitive form of Dutch barn used for storing hay.

Massive blocks of hard granite make a stern and uncompromising facade for the solid houses near Dolgellau, and everywhere is seen the unadorned plainness occasioned by an unyielding building material and relative poverty. Even the timber-framed house at Ruthin lacks the decorative infill frequently found in its English counterparts.

N' BRECON · POWYS

RUTHIN
CLYWD

WELSH slate was once a principal export. Much of London is roofed with it, but in its native country it is used in many other ways. The window in Llanidloes, Powys is a fine example, it has a wonderful undulating lintel made from cleaved slate and intruders will no doubt avoid using the spiked window sill to kneel upon. The crossed-over lintel at Bala is also distinctive and, like the wall below it, relies for its appearance on the thinness of the slates employed.

The Marches and north-east Wales are the principal areas in which the use of timber is prevalent. The dormer window in Ruthin is one of seven, stepped in three levels in a tall tiled roof. Its moulded barge board adds further to its charm, while close by, Gothic tracery and an oddly shaped porch refines an otherwise plain doorway. Most typically Welsh is the massive door near Dolgellau where rough blocks of granite surround a solid oak door devoid of any decoration.

LLANIDLOES · POWYS

RUTHIN · CLYWD

BALA
GWYNEDD

RUTHIN
· CLYWD ·

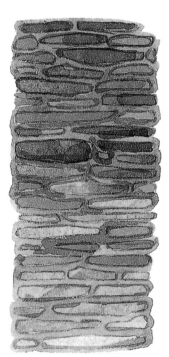

Nʳ HARLECH
GWYNEDD

Nʳ DOLGELLAU · GWYNEDD

A LONGHOUSE near BALA

THE Welsh longhouse has developed along similar lines to those of the north of England. This one, in north Wales, with its archway leading to the farmyard has a large chimney at the front, a feature also seen in Pembrokeshire and the West Country. The part of the building in which the farmer and his family live is whitewashed, a treatment which gives some protection against the elements and is often the only light in a rain-soaked lands-cape. Once again stone is the dominant material, the house walls are of granite and the roof is slate. Even the farmyard fence is made of slabs of slate held together with wire, a practice unique to this region. Hill farms like this are suffering from falling levels of subsidy offered by the European Community. Every cloud has a silver lining though, as with any luck, this agricultural depression may preserve from 'improvement' many of these fine buildings.

PONTGLAZIER 1873
PEMBROKESHIRE

TRECYNON · GLAMORGAN 1858

NOLTON HAVEN 1858
PEMBROKESHIRE

LLANDDEWI VELFREY 1820
PEMBROKESHIRE

CWMCAMLAIS 1835
BRECONSHIRE

PEINTRE BACH 1810
BRECONSHIRE

CHAPELS of the WELSH VALLEYS

THE title non-conformist was given to the Welsh churches which were established by those who failed to toe the line drawn by the 1662 Act of Uniformity. A subsequent Toleration Act of 1689 allowed freedom of worship but the desire not to appear aligned to the established English church continued. This led to the building of independent chapels that punctuate the villages of Wales. Their ever-increasing popularity in the eighteenth and early-nineteenth centuries led to the establishment of more and more denominations and often two or more chapels of different persuasions co-existed in one small village.

The earliest buildings were often converted from houses or barns and, when purpose-built, were truly vernacular. Examples of these are shown at Llanddewi, Cwmcamlair and Peintre Bach. However, as the nineteenth century progressed more decoration was introduced and, by the middle of the century, classical and baroque temples like that of Nolton Haven were becoming popular. Ironically today they are often being converted back into houses.

Perhaps the most renowned by-product of the chapel movement is the strong tradition of choral singing in Wales.

N^r ABERDARE · GLAMORGAN

The NORTH

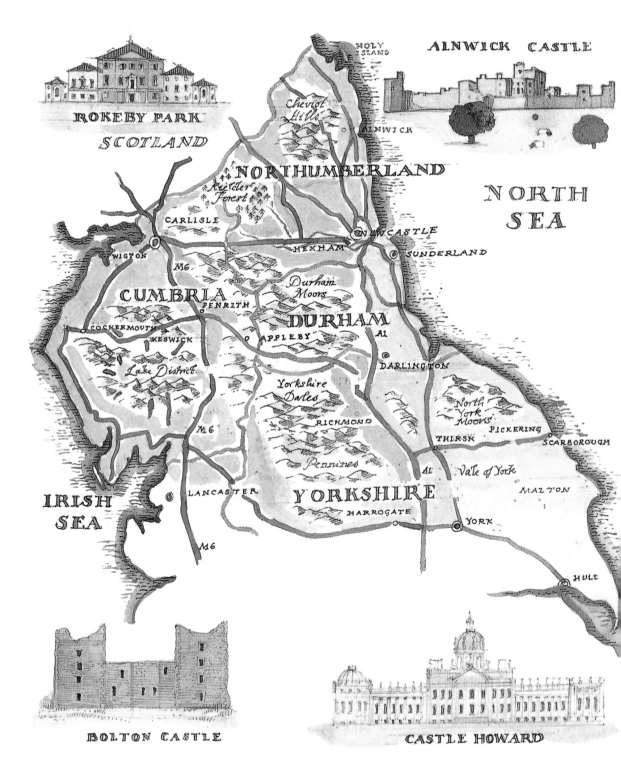

ROKEBY PARK

ALNWICK CASTLE

SCOTLAND

HOLY ISLAND

Cheviot Hills

ALNWICK

NORTHUMBERLAND

NORTH SEA

Kielder Forest

CARLISLE

NEWCASTLE

HEXHAM

WIGTON

SUNDERLAND

M6

CUMBRIA

Durham Moors

PENRITH

DURHAM

COCKERMOUTH

KESWICK

APPLEBY

A1

DARLINGTON

Lake District

M6

Yorkshire Dales

North York Moors

RICHMOND

PICKERING

THIRSK

SCARBOROUGH

Pennines

A1

Vale of York

MALTON

IRISH SEA

LANCASTER

YORKSHIRE

M6

HARROGATE

YORK

HULL

BOLTON CASTLE

CASTLE HOWARD

The NORTH

THE PENNINES dominate the North of England. Around this granite mountain spine, which runs north–south from Hadrian's Wall to Stoke-on-Trent and bisects the region, lies some of the most beautiful and dramatic landscape in Britain—the Lake and Peak Districts, the Yorkshire and Durham Moors and the Yorkshire Dales. Despite the diversity of scenery there is a strong sense of continuity in building styles. The use of hard stone and slate had led to a no-nonsense type of foursquare and squat building with simple cottages and modest farmhouses built of granite and sandstone.

Outside of the vernacular, of course, there is no shortage of grand buildings in the North of England which contains some of Britain's finest ecclesiastical establishments, such as the ruined abbeys of Rivaulx and Jervaulx and the massive and awe-inspiring Romanesque cathedral of Durham. Castle Howard, Harewood House and Chatsworth are reminders of the tremendous wealth and great estates of the aristocracy in the north.

The landscape of northern England is scarred by centuries of quarrying and mining; coal, lead, granite, slate and a rich variety of limestones and sandstones. In the clay-rich lowlands of North Cumbria many of the buildings are made of the local red and cream bricks with corners of dressed stone. The only other area where bricks are used to any great extent is the Vale of York, the flat country that runs south from the North York Moors to the Humber. Here the use of Dutch gables and fine moulded bricks and the size of the houses emphasizes the prosperity of this agricultural area and gives it more in common with neighbouring East Anglia than with the rest of the north.

To the west of the Pennines the Cumbrian lakes lie between steep mountain peaks. The stone buildings of the Lake District are often white-washed and roofed with local green slate. These are the cottages so familiar from the books of Beatrix Potter, whose beautiful watercolours have made this the quintessential English countryside for many people. Sadly, this very beauty has made the area too popular for its own good and the fells are now suffering from erosion not by wind and rain but from the feet of tourists.

Industry is inextricably linked to the landscape of northern England; in the sprawling cities of Manchester, Leeds and Sheffield and in grey deserted mining villages like Nenthead, near Alston, now stranded at the very top of the Pennines with no industry to sustain it. However, this industrial connection to the countryside is probably most surprising when one comes upon Colne, Burnley or Blackburn, lying in deep valleys and housing the original dark Satanic mills, while above them on either side rise wild hills covered with heather moorland stretching away until the next valley conceals another clutch of factories and back-to-back stone cottages.

FARM·BARDON MILL·HEXHAM

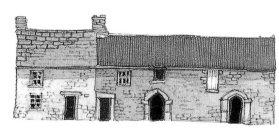

DUKESFIELD nr HEXHAM
NORTHUMBERLAND

ARKENGARTHDALE·YORKSHIRE

FIELD~BARN·CUMBRIA

RICHMOND·YORKSHIRE

COTTAGE Nr RICHMOND

DVRHAM

NEWBIGGIN·CUMBRIA

FARM nr WIGTON · CUMBRIA

HOUSE Nr BROUGH

EGTON · NORTH YORKS

ARKENGARTHDALE YORKSHIRE

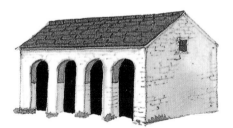

BARN near STANHOPE
DVRHAM

FARMHOUSE near APPLEBY

VIEWLEY · NORTHUMBERLAND

COTTAGE in NEWBIGGIN

STONE is the predominant building material in the North of England which is why so many old buildings have survived. However, the building material may outlive the use of the building. When a building is demolished, the stone—particularly blocks of dressed stone—will be reused, making it not uncommon to see finely detailed carving in the fabric of a relatively humble barn. The gothic doorways in the house at Dukesfield on the previous page may well have come from a grander building now demolished. As an alternative to demolition, a once-great structure may be adapted for other uses. The farm at Bardon Mill was once the gatehouse of a fortified manor but has since descended the social scale through smithy and farm building until now it serves only as the entrance to a later farmyard and its rooms are all unused.

The white barn near Stanhope is an unusual building with its tall and wide arches, and predates the open corrugated-iron Dutch barns of this century by a hundred years. The house in Richmond is shown in rear elevation to emphasize the arched gothic window which lights the staircase. This is a typical feature in the slightly grander houses of the area, see the example in Hexham opposite.

BLANCHLAND · HEXHAM

BARDON MILL,
NORTHUMBERLAND

NEWBIGGIN · CUMBRIA

WIGTON · CUMBRIA

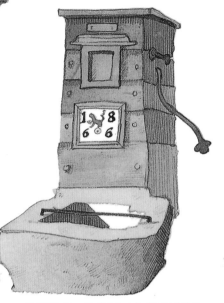

UPPER·DENTON·GILL
CUMBRIA

PUMP·ROMALDKIRK

BRANCHLAND
NORTHUMBERLAND

REDMAIN·CUMBRIA

HEXHAM

CUMBRIA

A LONGHOUSE in ARKENGARTHDALE

In the Yorkshire Dales or the Lake District among the neat landscape of field barns and stone walls you will see longhouses. The longhouse has become the dominant form of farmhouse throughout a great part of the upland North and in it, the farmer, his family and his animals are all housed beneath a common roof. The family home is at one end while the barn is at the other. The proportion of the buildings used for human habitation can expand and contract to suit the size of the family without major rebuilding work or extravagant use of buildings materials.

That is exactly what has happened in this example in Arkengarthdale in North Yorkshire. The barn side of the building is plain with simple plank doors and undressed stone walls. The house side is clearly divided, the walls have been rendered to keep out the damp and cold and to smarten up the place and the doorway is framed with a fine stone lintel into which a date has been carved. This might be the date of the building's construction but could equally well have been to mark a birth or marriage in the family.

Originally the entrance would probably have been in the centre of the building leading on to a cross-passage dividing the house from the barn. This house has developed in an organic way and, although it is in many ways haphazard—for example no two windows are the same—the effect of the whole group of buildings is thoroughly satisfying. The composition is made the more perfect by three hawthorn trees growing in front of the longhouse and shown in the drawing earlier in this chapter. They illustrate how important planting can be in the preservation of buildings of this sort. These thorns, shaped into neat compact trees by the wind and by grazing from beneath, are particularly suited to this landscape. They are as native to the countryside as the house is and the whole picture would lose its 'authenticity' and consequently much of its character if they were replaced with a neat cypress hedge.

SLIT WINDOW
IN REAR OF
BARN

FRONT DOOR

UNEQUAL SASH
& STONE SURROUND

REDMAIN CUMBRIA

The BORDERS

The BORDERS

ROM EARLIEST times, until the rebellion of
Bonnie Prince Charlie in 1746, skirmishes
and raids have punctuated the less than
cordial relations between the Scots and the English.
Since the Romans built Hadrian's Wall, and later
the Antonine Wall, all substantial houses in this
region have required a degree of fortification and
many of these fortified buildings, known as Piel
Towers, survive—from the Cheviot Hills in the east
to the Solway Firth in the west. The smaller houses
have survived less well. As has happened in many of
the poorer areas of Britain, buildings have been
dismantled so that their stone may be used for their
replacement.

The hilly landscape that dominates this area is
part heather covered and part poor grassland,
known as white ground. Until recently it was very
sparsely wooded but, in the last fifty years or so,
large areas have been forested, sadly mainly with
blanket planting of Sitka spruce. The largest of
these plantations is the Kielder Forest, most of
which is just south of the border in Northumberland. This is the largest man-made forest in Europe
and in it are submerged countless farms, cottages
and even villages. It lies like a fat green toad

dominating the surrounding countryside.

In the lowlands that cover the central part of
southern Scotland, the prominent building material is sandstone. The land is relatively flat and
fertile and is good for mixed farming, producing
good arable yields and lush pasture to fatten cattle
raised in the bleaker climate of the Highlands and
Islands. Neat, plain, symmetrical farmhouses front
well-maintained farms and low-built, often rendered cottages—with stone door frames and window frames and roofed in slate—cluster in the
villages.

One feature shared by much vernacular architecture of the Borders is the crow's-foot gable, made
of squared stones which produce a stepped profile.
The practice was developed to avoid cutting the
extremely hard local stone. Many of the buildings
have been harled (the Scottish form of rendering)
with roughcast and then painted, the only decoration being the colouring of the plain stone window
and door surrounds to contrast with the walls. A
village such as Culross in Fife, whose continuous
façades are painted in whites, pale creams and soft
pinks, is roofed in red pantiles. Its homogeneity is
reminiscent of the medieval hill towns of Tuscany.

GALASHIELS
BORDERS

DUMFRIES

GALASHIELS
BORDERS

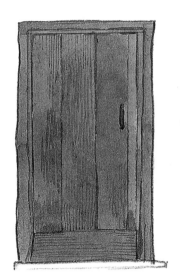

GIRVAN
DUMFRIES and GALLOWAY

EYEMOUTH

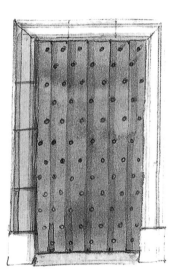

PEEBLES
BORDERS

CULROSS
FIFE

THE Border region is built on rock. There is very little timber available for building and bricks are extremely rare. Many old stone buildings have survived, such as the sixteenth-century Oakwood Tower in Selkirk which, with its sheer walls, steeply pitched slate roof and small windows, is typical of the tower-houses that are found all over Scotland. The circular kiln at East Linton in Fife was used to dry barley for malting.

Many buildings in the border region have walls of bare stone. A common practice is to render the walls with roughcast. As well as protecting a building against the elements, rendering adds a brightness to an otherwise bleak landscape as it allows the introduction of colour, not only white, but also warmer ochre and terracotta.

The house at Alloway in Ayrshire was lived in by Robert Burns and is the more comfortable Lowland equivalent of the bleak croft of the Highlands.

EAST·LINTON · FIFE

OAKWOOD ·SELKIRK

Nᴿ CRAIL · FIFE

Nr GATEHOUSE of FLEET
DUMFRIES and GALLOWAY

ALLOWAY   AYRSHIRE

CULROSS FIFE

MODEL FARMS

THE eighteenth century saw a tremendous upheaval in agricultural practices in Britain. The open field system, in which individual peasants cultivated strips divided from a larger field, was swept aside in the mania for enclosure; Act after Act was passed by Parliament from the sixteenth century onwards but the General Enclosure Act finally made it possible for landowners to develop their farms without recourse to law.

Parallel with this came a corresponding change in farm buildings. Most remarkable was the employment, for the first time, of architects such as Adam, Wyatt and Soane, who introduced 'polite' architecture to what had been vernacular agricultural buildings.

Sir John Soane's designs at Wimpole Hall make interesting use of local materials while imposing on them classical order. Castle Barn Farm at Badminton, designed by Thomas Wright, takes a more fanciful attitude. The Great Barn at Holkham in Norfolk was designed in 1790 by Samuel Wyatt for Coke, the great agricultural reformer. Finest of the medieval barns, Great Coxwell in Berkshire has some of the same grandeur but it was built to collect tithes owed to Beaulieu Abbey.

Nowhere were the theories of the new agriculture taken up so enthusiastically as in the Borders. Between 1760 and 1800 almost all of lowland Scotland was enclosed and model farms were built everywhere. A fine example, designed by Robert Adam at Kirkdale, is shown opposite.

PARK FARM · WIMPOLE · CAMBRIDGESHIRE

CASTLE·BARN BADMINTON, GLOUCESTERSHIRE

KIRKDALE ·KIRKUDBRIGHTSHIRE

TITHE BARN · GREAT COXWELL
BERKSHIRE

GREAT BARN·HOLKHAM · NORFOLK

145

The HIGHLANDS *and* ISLANDS

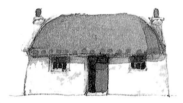

The HIGHLANDS *and* ISLANDS

THE HIGHLANDS of Scotland are the least populated region of Britain. Large parts of it are uninhabitable mountains and its comparative poverty has curbed major population expansion. Most important though were the infamous Highland clearances. From the end of the eighteenth century, the Lairds, who only two generations before had been the patriarchal chiefs of the Scottish clans, began to clear the clansmen from their farms. Influenced by life in Edinburgh and London, they were lured by the money that could be accrued by letting their land to sheep farmers from the south. Despite vociferous resistance, frequently violent, an unstoppable current of change drove the crofters from their land to make way for the new sheep walks. Countless villages were depopulated and their inhabitants either moved to marginal coastal land or to ships waiting in the harbours, bound for Canada and America.

So violent were these clearances that most houses were razed to the ground and now a church cemetery, or even a collection of boulders is often the only evidence of a vanished village. However, some crofts have survived, most noticeably in the Western Isles. In North Uist, in the Outer Hebrides, only a few of the original black houses (see overleaf), that so shocked the Victorian tourists, survive. These single-storey dwellings are built of stone, sometimes with double walls between which earth or peat is packed. The roofs are thatched with turf or heather and held down by a series of ropes that are anchored with rocks placed along the eaves. Photographs taken in the nineteenth century show plain stone walls presenting a bleaker impression than that obtained by rendering and painting.

In the third quarter of this century the economy of the Highlands has altered dramatically. Oil revenue from the North Sea oil fields has made Aberdeen a boom town, while fish-farming, grouse-shooting, deer-stalking and forestry have provided rural employment. Most infamous was the planting of the flow country near Caithness. A loophole in the British fiscal system allowed tax-free investment in a forestry project that would have turned hundreds of square miles of unspoilt wilderness into an unproductive and barren wasteland. Pressure from environmental groups has now closed the loophole before too much damage was done.

THE house in North Uist in the Outer Hebrides and the one near Inverness are examples of primitive crofts called black houses. Originally unpainted and with no windows, there would have been a central hearth and the floor would be rammed earth. The house in Argyll, which dates from the last years of the nineteenth century, is an example of a subsequent form of croft. The roof is slate, square and laid in a diamond pattern and the outbuildings are of corrugated iron, a typical use of the material.

The weather in this part of Britain can be bleak. The walls of the terrace at Portree in Skye have been rendered as protection against wind and rain and the granite and slate cottage at John O'Groats in Sutherland is low-lying to stand up against the winds.

Overleaf are shown typical elements of local buildings, such as door and window surrounds which illustrate the simple detailing which coped with such an intransigent material—although a religious need often produced the more elaborate carving of the Celtic cross.

SKIPNESS

COTTAGE · JOHN O GROATS SUTHERLAND

NORTH UIST

Nr INVERNESS

PORTREE - SKYE

CROFT in ARGYLL

NORTH UIST

NORTH UIST

IONA

Nʀ INVERNESS

Typical of the early tower-houses, Drum Castle in Aberdeenshire dates from the late thirteenth century. Its tall, sheer rubblestone walls rise to a shallow corbel and culminate in a crenellated parapet. The large window and adjacent buildings were added later. Castle Fraser, which was built in the late sixteenth century, has round, projecting turrets with steep conical roofs and is a fine model for

EILEAN DONNAN CASTLE
HIGHLANDS

DRUM · GRAMPIAN

CASTLE FRASER
GRAMPIAN

the Scottish baronial style. Inspired by the romantic vogue for highland life, this style was adopted across the world by nineteenth-century builders. The similarities between the appearance of Scottish castles and the French châteaux of the fifteenth and sixteenth centuries is due to the close relationship between Scotland and France in Tudor times, known as the 'Auld Alliance'.

GLOSSARY

IT IS almost impossible to discuss or describe a building without some knowledge of its component parts and for this one must be able to dissect it. The language of vernacular building is not one of overly technical terms. It is after all, by definition, a language spoken by builders who were working in a familiar idiom. However, one or two terms are quite confusing and often misunderstood—the ideal loop-hole for a bungling builder. It is worth finding out exactly what a builder means by a particular word as some rely on shaming you into not betraying your ignorance.

Although these pages are intended as a visual guide, and should be largely self-explanatory, there are some terms which need clarification:

WINDOWS which slide either from side to side or, more usually, up and down are called SASH windows. If they open from one or other hinged side they are then CASEMENTS. A window is made up of PANES or by LEADING or LATTICE.

The wall above a window is supported by a stone, wooden or brick LINTEL.

The arrangement of windows in the FACADE (front) or the REAR or SIDE ELEVATION of a building is sometimes referred to as FENESTRATION.

Wooden-framed buildings are supported by vertical POSTS and horizontal BEAMS.

The ROOF of a building is supported by RAFTERS. On it TILES and SLATES are PEGGED to BATTENS. THATCHED ROOFS of REED or STRAW are held in place by hazel RODS secured by split hazel BROACHES.

CHIMNEY POTS sit on top of a STACK.

MASONRY (stone) or brick is layed in COURSES divided by MORTAR.

Brick is layed in different BONDS; ENGLISH, FLEMISH, STRETCHER etc. Bond refers to the pattern made by the arrangement of HEADERS (short side of the brick) and STRETCHERS (long side) in a course of brickwork.

STONE is cut and carved to form MOULDINGS and DRESSINGS. If it is quarried but used rough and totally undressed it is called RUBBLE STONE. If cut into regular but rough blocks it is called SQUARED and if turned into smooth and perfectly regular rectangles, ASHLAR. If the stone or brick is covered in a cement mix it has been RENDERED.

On the next few pages are dissections of imaginary houses. They are composite buildings, none of which you would actually find and they include some grander architectural details since elements of these are often found in quite humble vernacular buildings.

WEATHERBOARDING

BRICK STRETCHER BOND

FLEMISH BOND

ENGLISH BOND

BRICK AND KNAPPED FLINT

BRICK AND ROUND FLINT

RUBBLE STONE

SQUARED STONE

TIMBER & BRICK NOGGING

TIMBER & PLASTER INFILL

TILE HANGING

ASHLAR - FINE CUT STONE

PANTILES

PLAIN TILES

SLATE

STONE

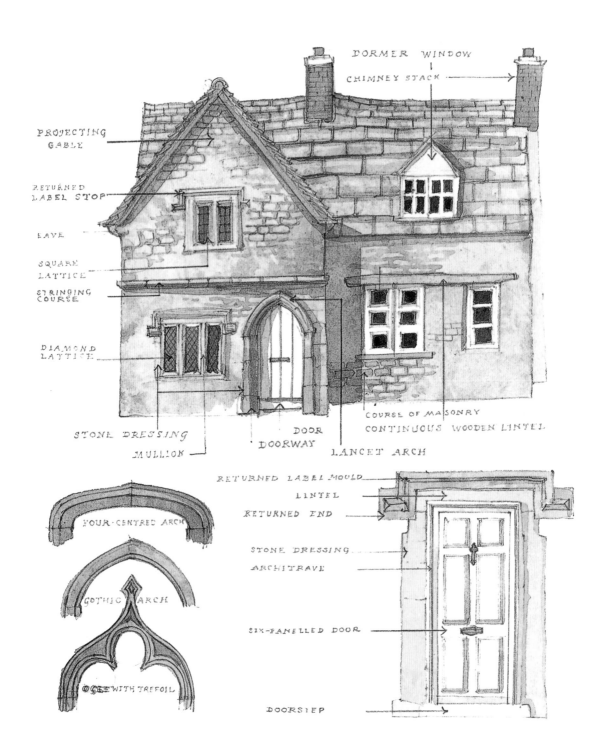

DORMER WINDOW

CHIMNEY STACK

PROJECTING GABLE

RETURNED LABEL STOP

EAVE

SQUARE LATTICE

STRINGING COURSE

DIAMOND LATTICE

STONE DRESSING

MULLION

DOOR

DOORWAY

LANCET ARCH

COURSE OF MASONRY

CONTINUOUS WOODEN LINTEL

FOUR-CENTRED ARCH

GOTHIC ARCH

OGEE WITH TREFOIL

RETURNED LABEL MOULD

LINTEL

RETURNED END

STONE DRESSING

ARCHITRAVE

SIX-PANELLED DOOR

DOORSTEP

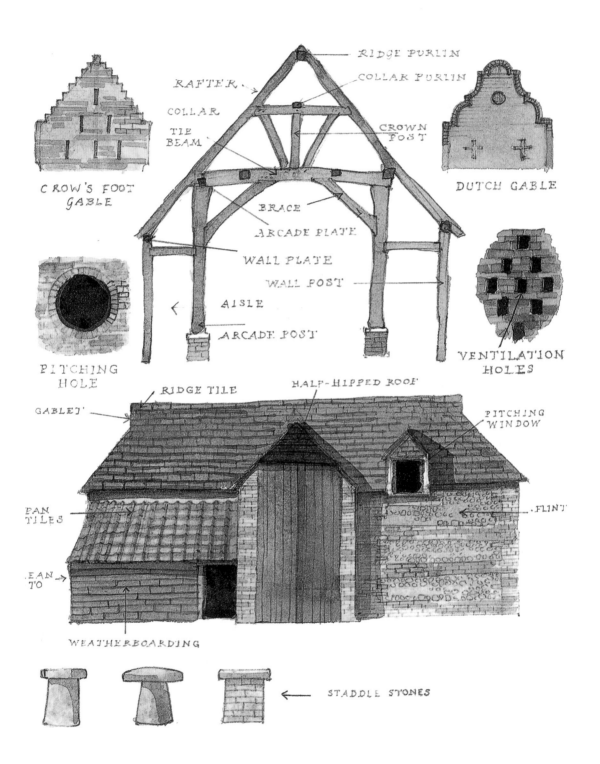

CROW'S FOOT GABLE

RIDGE PURLIN

COLLAR PURLIN

RAFTER

COLLAR

TIE BEAM

CROWN POST

DUTCH GABLE

BRACE

ARCADE PLATE

WALL PLATE

WALL POST

AISLE

ARCADE POST

PITCHING HOLE

VENTILATION HOLES

RIDGE TILE

HALF-HIPPED ROOF

GABLET

PITCHING WINDOW

PAN TILES

FLINT

LEAN TO

WEATHERBOARDING

STADDLE STONES

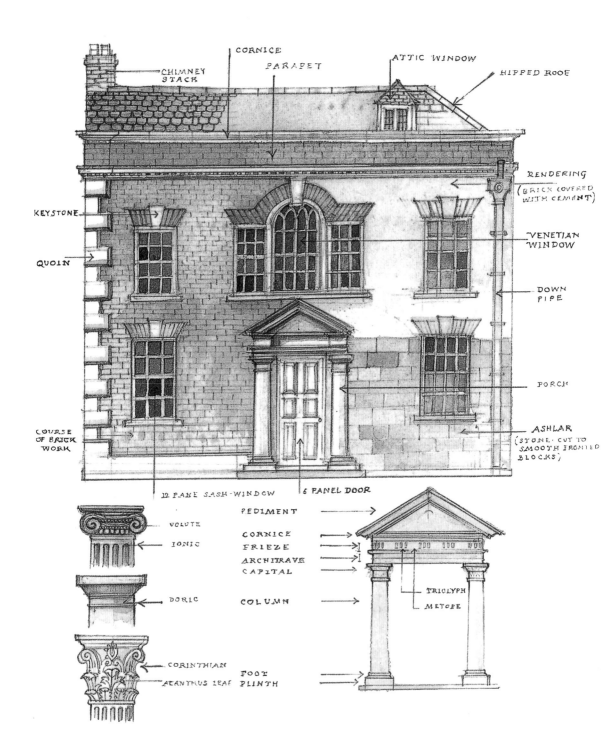

CORNICE

PARAPET

CHIMNEY STACK

ATTIC WINDOW

HIPPED ROOF

RENDERING
(BRICK COVERED WITH CEMENT)

KEYSTONE

VENETIAN WINDOW

QUOIN

DOWN PIPE

PORCH

COURSE OF BRICK WORK

ASHLAR
(STONE CUT TO SMOOTH FRONTED BLOCKS)

12 PANE SASH-WINDOW

6 PANEL DOOR

VOLUTE

IONIC

DORIC

CORINTHIAN

ACANTHUS LEAF

PEDIMENT

CORNICE

FRIEZE

ARCHITRAVE

CAPITAL

COLUMN

FOOT

PLINTH

TRIGLYPH

METOPE

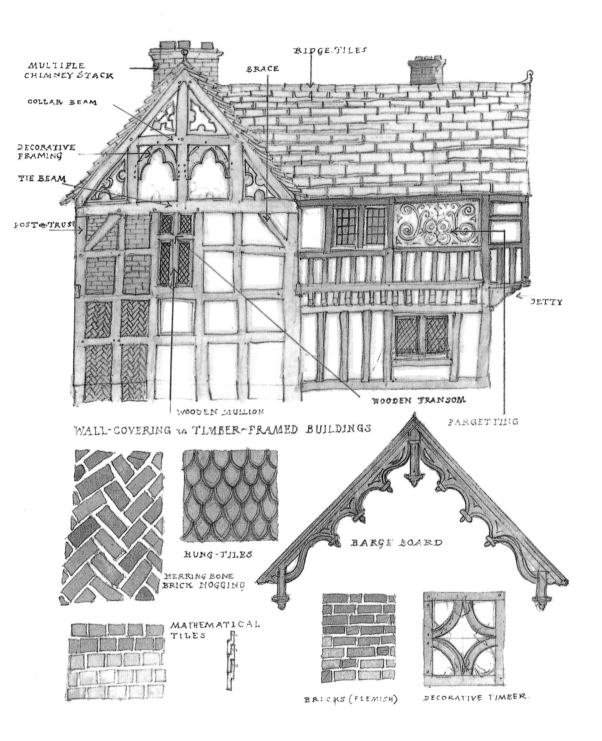

MULTIPLE CHIMNEY STACK

COLLAR BEAM

DECORATIVE FRAMING

TIE BEAM

POST or TRUSS

RIDGE·TILES

BRACE

JETTY

WOODEN MULLION

WOODEN TRANSOM

PARGETTING

WALL·COVERING in TIMBER-FRAMED BUILDINGS

HUNG-TILES

HERRING BONE BRICK NOGGING

BARGE BOARD

MATHEMATICAL TILES

BRICKS (FLEMISH)

DECORATIVE TIMBER

INDEX